The Power of Love

Copyright © 2013 Simone Boger

All rights reserved

All rights reserved. No part of this book may be reproduced in any manner without written permission except for quotations embodied in critical articles or reviews.

Book cover and illustrations
Shilo Shiv Suleman

Layout and Typesetting
Cris Lima

ISBN-13: 978-1494837440
ISBN-10: 1494837447

Simone Boger

The Power of Love
Returning to the Source

Illustrations
Shilo Shiv Suleman

Some day, after mastering winds, waves, tides and gravity, we shall harness for God the energy of love, and then, for the second time in the history of the world, man will have discovered fire.

Pierre Teilhard de Chardin
Toward the Future

Contents

Introduction 11
    The One 20
    Getting His Vibes 23
    Particle and Wave 27
    Love for Solitude 31
    In the Eye of the Storm 35
    Opening the Third Eye 38
    Silent Home 41
    Emptiness and Fullness 43
    Relationships 46
    Love Yourself to Love Another 50
    Being Connected – Exploring
        Relationships with God 53

Bhagwan ke Yaadgar – God's Memorials ... 59
    Parampita — The Father 60
    Divya Mata — The Divine Mother ... 63
    Karankaravanhar – The One who Acts
        and Works through Others 66

Param Shikshak — The Teacher 70
Patit Paavan — The Purifier and
  Healer of Hearts 73
Prem ka Sagar — The Ocean of Love
  and Cosmic Experiences 77
Divya Kratavya — The Divine
  Activity of the Creator 81
Gyan ka Surya – The
  Sun of Knowledge 84
Bholanath — The Lord of Innocence 88
Nyara — The Unique and
  Detached Observer 91
SatGuru — The True Guide 94
Sarvashaktiman — The Almighty
  Authority 97
Dharamraj — The Lord
  of Righteousness 100
Paras — The Alchemist 103
Bhagwan ka Avataran — The
  Incarnation of God 106
Nirakari — The Incorporeal 110
Piyu — The Beloved 113

Cause and Effect 117

The only way out is within 121
There is benefit hidden in everything 123
Traveling in Space and Light 125
Spiritual Healing 128
Going Deeper 131
Past Lives 136
Positive Vibrations 139

Walk your journey in Silence	141
Purity and Love	143
Becoming Yogis	146
Yaguia — the Sacrificial Fire	150
Their First Belief	151
Beginning Meditation	155
Tips for Meditation and Spiritual Development	157

About the Authors 163

Introduction

The reflections shared in this book have at their core a certain kind of love, the love we can attain from a connection with the Divine. Though not a conscious choice at first, having spiritual love as a subject emerged as the writing developed, almost as a sign to be followed.

Despite the innumerable crises we face today and the various connotations the very word "God" carries, we live in an incredible time for experiencing the power and beauty of the spiritual realm. It is up to us to rediscover the heart within the spirit, and by doing so, to learn how a direct relationship with the One remembered as the Mystery of mysteries becomes possible.

Most of us have our own concepts when it comes to the Divine. We have been thinking, listening and talking about him for ages. Yet, after so many years of teaching meditation, I have heard few people talking about spiritual attainments or inner fulfillment.

The exploration and sharing you will find in the next pages tries to bridge this gap. It is based on the perspective of Raja Yoga meditation, a practice that benefits mind and body, while opening up subtle channels in the soul. This is a method rooted in ancient Indian philosophy yet with a contemporary bent that makes it very practical and accessible to people of any age and culture.

I have purposely abstained from quoting complex teachings or academic studies, and have tried my best to share tested tips and yogic experiences which repeatedly return to one common expression. For we have to keep in mind that love is the language spoken by God.

Whenever we use the word yoga we tend to think of physical postures and breathing exercises as these have become almost synonymous with the term. Here, however, the word is used with respect to its roots – in a purely spiritual sense – to mean going beyond the physical aspects of life and reconnecting the inner self with the One.

As we know, high states of consciousness and insights can only be accessed first hand. Hopefully experimenting with the various aspects of spiritual knowledge might be of help in facilitating and inspiring the readers to become explorers themselves. For this, we only need genuine interest, some discipline and a clean heart.

By a clean heart I mean letting love and compassion guide our choices, until it becomes a habit. Everything else has been tried, and the more we have grown distant from our truth, the greater the loss we´ve come to feel. It is time for us to experiment with the qualities that belong to our core being, for they can, in turn, lift us to the highest orb of Light – to the very Source which fills the soul with light and love.

By all means they try to hold me secure, those who love me in this world. But it is otherwise with your love which is greater than theirs, for you keep me free. Lest I forget them, they never venture to leave me alone. But day after day pass by and you are not seen. If I do not call you in my prayers, if I do not keep you in my heart, your love for me keeps waiting for my love.

Rabindranath Tagore – *Free Love – Gitanjali*

Love is the greatest force in existence; it is the heartbeat of life. It is the most elevated flow of feelings and the purest energy within our souls. It simultaneously radiates and attracts, transforming whatever it meets, melting or washing up areas of darkness. No wonder all of us wish to remain in the bliss of this experience. And it is in the arena of relationships where we are most likely to seek it.

Yet, the more we humans modernize, the less available heartfelt, spontaneous love seems to be.

Have we missed some point along the journey or is this just the expected outcome of values and interests in a material age?

As I began exploring this subject in meditation seminars, it startled me how people responded to the experience of pure, spiritual love. A few hours of inspired sharing, reading and guided meditation was enough for an opening of hearts and unprecedented experiences. It made me see that the time is now ripe for us to dive deep into the Ocean.

If on the one hand we witness rapid transformations and loss in many areas, on the other, we now definitely have more access to the beauty and power of the spiritual dimension. It is up to us to see this time as an opportunity to experiment and get replenished with those qualities and experiences we internally lack.

And there are ways we can do this, for example, by sharing. Most people are now seeking to fulfill their basic needs, like peace of mind and affection. As a result, our culture has become one of grabbers and go-getters. Even though most of us know that it is by giving that we receive, we sometimes hesitate in reaching out to others.

Yet once we take the initiative, these little acts in our daily lives bring immediate benefit. It may be a smile, a helping hand, a phone call or an empathetic ear you lend to someone. It may even be just a thought – one filled with good wishes or compassion.

The other way requires more in terms of method, but it is far more powerful. Here I mean experiencing love and other qualities by going to their very Source. Having our minds connected directly to the mind field of God has the effect of filling our inner being with clarity, strength and enthusiasm. It feels like a kind of rebirth.

For ages, spiritual love has been the focus and fuel of mystical experiences. This is the kind of love that is unlimited and leaves us with a sense of fulfillment that is nourishing and empowering. We need, however, to learn how to dive deeply in order to emerge with jewels that can be found only beneath the surface.

From the beginning of my meditation practice, my focus has been to experiment with the varied aspects, roles and faces of God. Rather than being devotional or ritual practices, these were experiences based on knowledge. Whatever major changes I went through, whether internal or external, were accompanied by the underlying feeling of his presence and inspiration.

Once the flame of the soul was ignited, the love of the spirit kept burning in the heart. I now realize that this was not the fortune of a lifetime, but that it came rather as a result. The quest was long, yet the needs of the spirit were finally met. I now know that meeting the Beloved is the path itself.

I thought that my voyage had come to its end at the last limit of my power, that the path before me was closed, that provisions were exhausted and the time had come to take shelter in a silent obscurity. But I find that your will knows no end in me. And when old words die out on the tongue, new melodies break forth from the heart; and where the old tracks are lost, new country is revealed with its wonders.

Rabindranath Tagore – *Closed Path—Gitanjali*

A few years ago I developed a condition and for some months felt I was on the brink of leaving. Though I sensed I was spiritually protected and loved, there were things to be faced and understanding to be gained. I could see the reason why I had to go through it, but that did not make it less of a challenge. The turning point came with the support and very practical helping hand of God.

It is better if I clarify from the beginning: the One I understand and experience as the Highest Being is a pure, peaceful and powerful consciousness. He has no human form, physical or subtle. No head, arms or legs; just a point-form of conscious light.

If there is one thing most people know about God, it is that despite centuries of discussions and theological debates, his nature and personality remain elusive. This might be because of his level of subtlety. While it may be easy to remember him, we require a refinement of mind, intellect and physical energies in order to absorb his vibrations.

Because life through the physical senses has become so deeply rooted in our nature, we have lost the art of experiencing pure awareness. God's love and kindness manifests in waves of rarefied, subtle light and feelings. To catch them, we need to gauge our minds first.

We might have felt that things related to the spiritual dimension often have a dreamy, almost unreal quality to them. We might also have felt that we have seen and heard so much without experiencing. We know how God's existence has been questioned, distorted and manipulated to fit selfish or even negative purposes. Yet we cannot deny that he continues to be the single most remembered and called for presence, no matter in what language, form or attribute.

Coming back to that risky condition, what then followed was a sequence of small miracles that not only deepened my gratitude, but opened up a new chapter in my own self-transformation. The thought of writing about spiritual experiences emerged because of that. Before, this was a treasured but private relationship.

I was in my early twenties when meditation became part of my daily routine. The powerful insights I was fortunate to have, along with a sense of self-discipline and renunciation, helped me build a strong inner foundation that shaped whatever was to follow. And life kept bringing a variety of challenges and detours.

It is helpful for us to understand that when it comes to transforming consciousness, part of the game is that we will certainly meet inner and outer resistance. Situations and obstacles will keep coming — in fact, at times they will be even stronger than before, as if trying to pull us down or drain our carefully built inner reservoir. I came to accept opposition as part of the process of change. Things have to come to be overcome. Plus, they are also testers of our understanding and a chance to exercise our inner powers.

Yet, deep spiritual experiences are transformative and leave marks that no time, situation or person will ever be able to erase. In retrospect, I see that the love I found was really the one I had been longing for. Deep, supportive and fulfilling; like flights taking the soul beyond the constraints and limitations of everyday life. As the inner battery continues to be recharged, life is becoming more meaningful and valuable.

The One

It is the inner eye that sees God
The physical eyes cannot see him
It is the eye of experience that knows and recognizes the One
And it is the heart that wishes to stay in his company
And let him guide our life.

Dadi Janki

Our story is that of soul connection. It is the ancient tale of being apart and together, of searching and finding, only to lose the other once again. Many of us have been through the quest before and may have had deep experiences that are just waiting to be re-awakened. Our spiritual past is in fact our soul story, which may be compared to a journey extending and unfolding through births and rebirths—death being only an interlude, where one is conscious yet temporarily free from the physical vehicle.

Like us, God is also a soul, who is perfectly capable of hearing and responding to our inner feelings. Being conscious and without a body means our communication has to happen on another level.

Because he lives in another dimension and reality, beyond this field of action, he does not "read" or understand situations in the same way we do, through the senses. Maybe this is why he has been called *Abhogta*; "living beyond the joys and effects of actions". Being incorporeal also means he cannot get involved in the games we play with each other.

This, however, does not imply that he cannot play a role with us. Though hidden and incognito, he is free and able to act, inspire and sustain us. He may give us subtle help when necessary—provided we seek and are able to receive it. His activities are considered the most mysterious and at the same time the highest. Major religions and spiritual paths have centered around his figure.

We could picture God as the most renowned actor as well as director of this "drama" we call life. Because his part is played so silently, as if behind the scenes, he often seems to be out of reach. This is why we need to learn to delve into his subtlety. This has in fact been at the basis of ancient yoga and all mystical paths. The meditative experience is essential in this respect, for it allows us to transcend, even if temporarily, the density and limitations of corporeal existence.

In the last few decades, meditation has grown in popularity, but it is still not practiced on a large scale. Ours is a world that thrives on activity, on action and its results, and meditation means we put ourselves in a quieter and more receptive mode. Extraordinary experiences may be just around the corner, but they require from us an internalized approach to life and an attention to detail.

Meditation is about experiencing the most subtle reality underlying life. It is also a means of exploring and promoting internal growth and creativity. When we meditate, there is always something new to be experienced.

Getting His Vibes

As the One who carries out many tasks, God has been remembered in many forms, with a number of names and titles related to his subtle activities. I especially like the ancient Sanskrit name of Shiva, which fittingly describes both his "point" of light form and his "benevolent" qualities.

Truth and love are universally remembered as God's main attributes, together with purity, mercy and peace. One I've grown to understand and appreciate is *Praneshwar*; the Giver of Life or vital energy. It reminds me that in the spiritual realm, miracles are possible.

The Highest Being has a mind that is always constant, emanating vibrations in the highest frequency. These vibrations reach us as waves of subtle yet potent energy, originating in his pure and loving "heart". To catch and absorb his penetrating power, however, we need to have a basic understanding of spiritual reality and its laws.

Connecting with or remembering God is a matter of feelings and is therefore very personal. Still, there is a method for tuning in directly to his frequency, which works a little like operating a radio. In this example, if you only have an AM radio you cannot expect to tune in to FM stations. Radio frequency bands vary according to the types of electromagnetic signals they emit.

Similarly, we also have a subtle inner receptor that makes use of thoughts to both emit and catch thought vibrations. The brain is but the control room and the physical device of the subtle and most wonderful operator called "the soul".

To tune in to a more refined mind wave, we require a refinement of our own thoughts and feelings, which means we need to select and at times filter what we constantly feed our minds. Whatever thoughts we radiate continue to create and sustain our energy field, impacting the self and other minds. Whether we are conscious of this or not, we constantly create an atmosphere around us through our thought waves. We have not only a receptor inside, we are also transmitters.

Now, imagine God's thoughts as the highest and purest vibrations traveling across this vast Universe. Clearly our inner chatter — the "AM radio" — will not be able to catch his frequency. Have you ever seen an image of ordinary thought patterns measured in the brain by an EEG?

So, it is a question of giving some attention to refining our thoughts, and this requires some effort. To tune in to powerful waves of peace and love and make the most of the experience, we need, in a way, to upgrade our energy first. To do this, we have to bring some lightness into our being, even if only a little, and while in the middle of chaos. In terms of tuning in, we are the ones who have to do it first.

The good thing about God is that he seems so happy with the slightest effort we make in his direction. One step from us and he will walk all the way to meet us. The magnet of his generous heart can pull us up even when we are a little rusty. All we need is to remember him with sincerity, patience and depth.

This refinement of our physical and mental energies also works to take us back to inner stability. This means we become open to creating thoughts and feelings that are purely related to nurturing our deep self and others. It means consciously producing the good wishes we expect others to have. This changes our vibrations. The purer our thoughts, the lighter and stronger we feel. The more peace, joy and kindness we experience, the easier it is for our mental fields to be free and powerful enough to catch higher spiritual vibrations. It is a question of energy: of like attracting like. People usually say that opposites tend to attract, but in the spiritual dimension, the more alike we are the closer we become.

Essentially, deep states of meditation can put us in contact with the emanating powerhouse of unconditional love and strength. This disposition or mindset of loving remembrance exists in the hearts of all faiths and is also the basis of spiritual yoga. It is this loving, receptive attitude that can bring us a multitude of qualities and experiences directly from the Source. Love is therefore both the attraction and the purpose of a relationship with the Divine.

Particle and Wave

Try to lead your thoughts into that dimension science calls subatomic and you will be mesmerized. None of our usual references and measures will work there, for this is a "world" ruled by the power of mind fields and the quality of thoughts produced by them.

This means that even if you can see nothing, you can still have experiences in a manner similar to the way you experience a feeling. The more you train your mind to do this, the easier it becomes. It is as if you develop an inner device that guides you through that realm.

For a meditator this is important because the closest we can get to God and the highest mental service happens in the invisible. The basis for this is the practice of becoming bodiless — of "going beyond". This exercise makes all the difference if we are willing to have close encounters. Direct experience is actually the only means we have of grasping God's individuality and knowing he is truly there for us.

We have recently been hearing a lot about developments in quantum physics and the quest for the most fundamental particles. A huge accelerator has been built in Europe to induce tiny fractions of atoms to collide in the hope that scientists may observe what so far has only been visible in mathematical projections. One of these particles popped up recently, a tiny spark that flashed into existence for a fraction of a second. Some called it "the God particle".

I was amazed by the efforts of these highly qualified minds working in collaboration to get a glimpse of such flimsy dots as well as by hearing some people believe they could get closer to proving God's existence. At the same time, I had a feeling that something was being missed.

Despite the fact that it was truly a great achievement and all the hype around it, it seemed to me that this giant underground lab could only succeed as far as detecting the fundamentals of the space or field in which we are all immersed. From the perspective of a yogi—or anyone familiar with the spiritual dimension—no such enterprise, no matter how advanced, will ever be able to scrutinize God's own being. The only device that serves this purpose is that very thing we all possess, yet are in much need of refining.

Here we enter the territory of direct experience. As we learn to focus inwards and get used to stabilize mind and intellect, we concentrate energy in a point inside the brain. This is the region of the frontal chakra, which get energized and activated by concentrating on the inner self.

The more we get in touch with the inner soul, the more we feel in control of our thinking. In fact, there comes a point we feel no need to think; we are released in the experience of deep inner silence. We are opened to the reality and power of pure awareness.

From this stage of soul consciousness, we can perceive the vibrations, the presence of another Light. We get the chance to connect with the light of the Supreme Soul.

God's form is that of a tiny dot, and that indeed is the original form of all conscious beings — an invisible spark of light. Whereas we humans need to be involved in layers of energy bodies to live in this material world, the form of the soul remains a point of light.

God, however, maintains this form for all time, as he is never born into a human body. He is always, eternally, just a Point of Light — the most elevated and powerful conscious Being. No wonder all religions remember him as Light.

Yet, this is a Being, not merely a zero point — which means he is alive and conscious, and can therefore connect and in his own way respond to our thoughts and feelings. His being radiates energy, as waves in an ocean, which reaches us as energizing, powerful and blissful vibrations.

These waves can be felt by trained minds; they can touch and transform us in a very unique way. For this reason, God has been called *Bindu* — the Point, as well as *Sindhu* — the Ocean. While he may be just a tiny soul, his light expands in radiant waves of peace, love and a variety of powers.

His very subtle and transcendent light can be received and absorbed once we are focused on the same wavelength. His radiant presence is being perceived by thousands of contemporary yogis in all corners of the planet. It is happening now at this transition of ages.

In fact, this is a very favorable moment for God´s true nature to be accessed and known through direct experience. No wonder science is trying to go deeper and deeper into the invisible, for this is where the greatest treasure lies.

So, no machine, no matter how sophisticated, will ever be able to find a God particle because this is the task of the human soul. It is a matter of connecting, as if he is just a thought away. We only need to focus our minds and reach him with the wings of our hearts.

Love for Solitude

Accept me, my lord, accept me for this while.
Let those orphaned days that passed without you be forgotten. Only spread this little moment wide across your lap, holding it under your light. I have wandered in pursuit of voices that drew me yet led me nowhere. Now let me sit in peace and listen to your words in the soul of my silence. Do not turn away your face from my heart's dark secrets, but burn them till they are alight with your fire.

Rabindranath Tagore – *Lover's Gift and Crossing*

"Think about this: you don't have a soul — you are a soul. What you have is a body."

Although knowing that we are souls may sound simple and true, there is more to it than just a liberating realization. In Raja Yoga meditation, the first thing we practice is getting in touch with the inner self, that part of us that knows the truth of existence. We learn how to concentrate and connect to our core — the eternal, conscious soul.

Those who enjoy introspection and find it refreshing to calm the endless inner chatter will find it easier to come close to the core of the self. It is a worthwhile effort, for it is in the essence of our being that peace, strength and love are to be found.

Despite knowing this, most of us have lost the taste for exploring the cool waters of calm and inner rest. Even our leisure means more activities—be it reading, listening to music or watching a film. All this is fine—it brings us happiness. But try to be quiet and in your own company and the mind will probably become restless, wishing to do something. Sure, the role of the mind is to think, yet we can always choose what and how to think. Because we no longer have the ability to be with the self, we end up losing precious gifts.

Being in solitude can also be a good way of checking our degree of self-esteem and self-worth. It is an opportunity to find out how we feel in our own company—does it feel comfortable or is there often longing for company and activity?

There is a story about ancient deities and how they churned the ocean as if to turn plain water into nectar or something precious. Another symbolic image shows them holding a spinning wheel with a finger. Both stories have a connection with the practice of deep reflection—with spinning our thoughts—for the purpose of strengthening one's mind and extracting meaning.

This is actually the role of spiritual knowledge, which is the basis of meditation. Contemplating spiritual truths is not a mere cerebral activity but an exercise of intellect that empowers the mind and may bring us wisdom over time.

By contemplating eternal truths, one develops a kind of reasoning that is not linear, that makes use of and develops qualities like inspiration, intuition and creativity. It also uses associations and correspondences that appear in a tangible way in one's life. We discover that it is not only the inner and outer worlds that reflect each other, but that our past has a lot to do with our present and that the higher dimensions find similarities in the ones below. Our intellects get sharpened by learning to look within as well as by reading signs and lessons that continue to emerge in our daily lives.

In case you might want to try—just for a moment—check what kind of thoughts and feelings you produce when trying stabilizing your mind. Give yourself the chance to focus on those thoughts for a few minutes, and take notes if you feel they are important.

The more we are able to expand our thoughts to include those things that are of no immediate concern and are not related to our mundane reality, the more our vision broadens.

Spiritual matters pertain to an unlimited territory. As we begin to sort out our thoughts, we feel a new kind of satisfaction as well as a feeling of being "in soft control", like a master. It then becomes easier to cultivate self-respect and inner kindness, and this will be expressed in relationships. When in a state of inner peace, our hearts expand to include others. Over time, our minds become more free and content, and they become a fertile soil for spiritual experiences.

Try to feed your mind with thoughts that make it light and that are related to spiritual understanding—you will see that they not only inspire but also generate energy and power of concentration. You can do it whenever your mind is free; you don´t need to sit or wait for a certain time of day.

Having love for solitude is an easy way of cultivating emotional stability and making a friend of your mind. This is the first step for rewarding experiences in meditation.

In the Eye of the Storm

All that really matters is how one lives one's life. Living will begin to achieve its own purpose when one's outer life becomes motivated, guided and balanced by the fruits of one's inner findings.

Paul Brunton – *Secret India*

Most of us sense that we are presently crossing rough waters. We live in a period of transition, a confluence of ages, when all structures—nature, economy, relationships—seem at best fragile, making people uncertain about the future. As imbalance increasingly becomes the norm, more people are feeling physically or emotionally battered, suffering one or another kind of internal pressure. In this scenario we may well realize that most of our supports are but temporary and that developing inner strength is something we might want to consider doing.

From a spiritual perspective, we are going through a rebirth—a renaissance—and therefore we have lessons to learn and things to let go. The old personality, based on a sense of false self, or ego, must die, together with other forms of vicious habits we carry within. The challenge is enormous and we need help and guidance in the process. A better, perfected world can only be brought about by perfected human beings. Our energy has to change and so do our inner motivations.

If you think connecting with God is for saints or the religious-minded, consider the benefits of attaining a source of stability and positivity, one that never runs dry. There might well come a time when people will no longer be able to provide for us. We will either be spiritually empowered and able to lend a hand to others, or we will be in the endless queue of those who are in need. By relating to the One remembered throughout the ages as "the Source", we can experience the love and support that is our birthright.

The unique thing about a relationship with God is that we gain inner powers that can be accumulated if we know how to care for them. We develop qualities like discernment, tolerance, courage and cooperation.

Meditation is not just a sitting experience—it gives us vital energy and clarity that can be used to develop new abilities and build inner strength.

People normally stock water and food when they know a hurricane is coming. This connection gives us that lifeline in moments of crisis; it is like having a stock that can be of use whenever the need arises.

Opening the Third Eye

"Be a soul as a living star"; "I am a soul... a star of gold..."

Pyramid texts – 904 and 886-9

Soul consciousness is the first step, so we always begin by stabilizing the mind. And we do that by connecting our thoughts with the inner self. There are certain thoughts that, because they are true, produce vibrations that pacify the mind. A quieter mind is all we need to begin meditation.

As we focus within, we can picture the self as a spark of light within the brain. We begin by remembering the conscious being that produces thoughts and feelings. We identify with the soul, the life within, and in those minutes we forget about our physical identity and everything related to it.

This is necessary because it is the immaterial self, as pure consciousness, that will both enter and experience the spiritual dimension. As we practice connecting with the inner self, qualities that are helpful for stabilizing the mind will begin to emerge. It is like pressing the button of conscious awareness.

The soul is immortal and exists independently from physical supports. It travels from body to body in its journey through time, carrying its life stories and personality traits as subconscious baggage. Its original qualities are purity, peace, love, knowledge and bliss.

As Pierre Teilhard de Chardin once remarked, "We are not human beings having a spiritual experience, we are spiritual beings having a physical experience."

If you're a visual type of person, you may want to start your meditation by picturing a point of light in the screen of your mind. As you concentrate on the self, behind your forehead, you might feel a surge of energy flowing up through your spine, similar to mercury rising in a thermometer. This concentration is unique in its capacity for aligning our energy field.

Have thoughts that will create genuine interest for continuing with your exploration and concentration. Thoughts like "Who am I, deep within?" or "What is it like being a spark of consciousness within this physical vehicle?"

Hold on to the thoughts, with no pressure, but with feeling, until they become experiences like "I am a peaceful soul", "I am an imperishable light", or "I am a master of this body."

The experience of soul consciousness gives wings to the soul. As you become more used to the practice, it will become easier to concentrate on the seat of awareness, on your higher self. You will then not only recognize yourself as a soul—you will feel it.

You'll also gain more clarity, perception and intuition. With constant practice and study, you'll get the chance to know your many traits, both conscious and subconscious. Connecting with the elevated self also allows a variety of beautiful memories and feelings to resurface. We get to know our strengths, virtues and talents. Once our "third eye" begins to open, we see and understand ourselves and others in a new light.

The Soul operates through three faculties:

Mind: Thoughts, Emotions, Imagination, Feelings, Sensations, Humors;

Intellect: Thoughts, Memory, Association of Ideas, Judgment, Decision, Will Power, Discernment, Options;

Sanskaras (subconscious mind): Memories, Talents, Instincts, Habits, Learning, Baggage, Beliefs.

Silent Home

It was a dimension of light; a space where we souls resided as if floating in a state of inner fulfillment. Without a body, the soul experienced deep inner silence. There was no impulse of action, no necessity for thoughts. There was peace.

Just as the physical world exists in an element called *akash*, or ether, similarly, the highest subtle realm exists in a principle or substance called *Akand Jyoti Maha Tattwa* — divine infinite light. This is our original home. It has been remembered as *Nirvana* — the realm beyond sound, and as *Brahmand* — the land of subtle light.

This dimension extends far beyond the limits of outer space. While resting on the highest region, the soul has no mental or sensory experiences, nor is it lost or dissolved in what seems like an ocean of diffuse light. It is a place of absolute silence.

Before they manifest, our inner qualities are latent, as if awaiting a clue—the right moment to begin playing our roles on this world stage.

Emptiness and Fullness

Enough with such questions!
Let silence take you to the core of life.
All your talk is worthless
When compared to one whisper of the Beloved.

Jalal ad-Din Rumi – *One Whisper of the Beloved*

People speak about living in the present as an ideal state of consciousness. Yet to live and enjoy each moment we first have to be "full", otherwise it is the nature of the mind to wander some place or another. It might be real needs or just unnecessary thoughts that keep ringing inside.

What then makes us full? What gives us a permanent sense of satisfaction, stability and self-dignity? Qualities, virtues and spiritual experiences are not only the means for replenishing the inner self but also the basis of a harmonious life. There is an Indian saying about a full bucket being able to resist the strongest storms, as opposed to an empty one, carried away by the slightest winds.

Many years ago, when I was beginning to meditate regularly, I went to a friend's house. When you get used to soul consciousness, you become more sensitive to the vibrations of places and people. It is almost like you can "catch moods" in the atmosphere.

That friend was a quantum physics professor and a disciplined Zen meditator. Because of his genuine dedication, his meditation room was already filled with vibrations of silence. The atmosphere was already there, and so it was easier for concentration and meditation to take its course. Back home that evening I was curious and tried to figure it out. I used to have the experience of silence in my own practice, so what was the difference in that?

I opened my notebook randomly and read a few lines on silence. It immediately dawned on me that what I had just experienced was "emptiness", which is a healthy cleaning up of the mind and the vibrations released by that state. It was also clear that I was used to a different kind of silence.

Usually I sit in meditation knowing how I feel internally and often with the aim of experiencing whatever I am lacking at that moment. If I am restless or tired I will go for peace and calm; if I feel a bit down for some reason I will set my thoughts on understanding and a happier mood; and so on.

But underlying these experiences is always something extra, for in those minutes that my mind finally gets merged into stillness, a sweet energy has already surrounded me. It is at this point that I can deeply feel the embracing warmth, the lovely feeling of fulfillment that emerges with the gift of God´s invisible presence.

From that day on, I could understand what ancient Indian culture meant by fullness or plenitude, and the meanings of symbols, like the full moon, which are but signs of spiritual attainments. It was a beautiful way of learning.

Relationships

You have made me known to friends whom I knew not, You have given me seats in homes not my own, You have brought the distant near and made a brother of the stranger. I am uneasy at heart when I have to leave my accustomed shelter, I forget that there abides the old in the new, and that, there also, You reside. Through birth and death, in this world or in others, wherever You lead me, it is you, the same, the one companion of my endless life who ever links my heart with bonds of joy to the unfamiliar. When one knows you, then no one is a stranger, no door is shut. Oh, grant me my prayer—that I may never lose the bliss of the touch of the One in the play of many.

Rabindranath Tagore – *Old and New* — *Gitanjali*

From a spiritual perspective, close relationships are never casual encounters. Whoever we meet in our daily lives has a good chance of being an old companion, and our being together in the present often has to do with the continuation of a hidden plot. The more we get in touch with our inner selves, the easier it becomes to discern the deeper meaning of our close relationships and to understand why we may tend to attract a particular type of person or find ourselves in patterns that keep repeating. We also sense that the more stable we are in our highest selves and the more connected with God, the more we are able to live and express our best qualities with others.

Like other traits we are born with, the intensity and depth of our feelings is unique to ourselves as individuals and is connected with a past that we cannot see or understand. Our lives are designed in such a way as to always offer us opportunities to express our positive potential and to develop and grow whatever is lacking. However, our purest feelings often happen to be blocked by inner traumas or weaknesses we know little about, as they have their roots in our subconscious minds. These may in turn become blockages on the path of spiritual development and realization. We all have singular stories behind what are seen externally as limitations, and this calls for greater compassion and respect in relation to ourselves and others. People are never only the image they project, and the tip of the iceberg is a good image for the stories we unknowingly carry. Nature is wise in that we are only aware of what is needed in order to deal with present issues. However, we have to keep in mind that this is a period of spiritual awakening, and our hidden aspects will naturally be made conscious in some way or another.

When it comes to the subject of love, we all respond to the simple truth that love begets love. It is in the expression of spontaneous affection and positivity that our feelings can expand and the beat of love can return to our hearts.

It is therefore of immense help if we do not fear but instead try to understand what needs to be cleared and healed in relation to our innermost feelings. As we make the effort to bring light to whatever is unconscious or unclear, we begin to experience that quality or power that resurfaces from the ashes of old traits and attitudes.

For example, there may be strength or determination beneath anger. Healing means realizing that there are mental habits that get in the way of our happiness and removing those blocks we've been using as false or temporary props so that there is mental space for our pure energy to flow again. We need that mental space, otherwise old thoughts and mental attitudes will always find a way of interrupting inner growth.

So, the more we genuinely accept that there is something to be changed, the more we will find help and support coming our way. To heal whatever is hurting or missing in the self we will need courage and spiritual assistance. This is a lifetime journey, yet one which is always rewarding.

Becoming spiritually awakened is an ongoing process that has to do with having a rich inner life and having our capacity of giving expanded to benefit others. By connecting our minds with the One, our hearts begin to heal, for we finally have a permanent and stable source of love and support. Sharing then becomes a means of increasing our happiness and fortune.

Love Yourself to Love Another

In our time, we have grown used to thinking of romance as the highest expression of love, as in the case of passion. This is probably connected with intensity of feeling and the fact that it does enable us to go beyond—even if only temporarily—the focus on the self. Heartfelt love may however also be present in parent and child relationships, in true friendships or in the feelings of deep awe and reverence of mystics.

My esoteric friends tell of invisible karmic bondages pulling the ties of passionate love. Think about it and it seems reasonable to assume that whoever or whatever you let your thoughts and energy be obsessively occupied with may actually mean something. This may be the reason why the ancients were so careful about bonding.

What often happens when the fire of passion subsides is that one is then faced with the real situation—with both the positives and the flaws of the self and the other person. For some it is at this point that a true loving relationship can begin developing, if both sides are mature enough to grow in respect, tolerance and mercy. Unfortunately, such relationships are rare. We need to understand karmic dynamics if we want to have a deeper look at this vast, endless subject. Many close relationships are indeed our meeting old issues and having the opportunity to make things right.

Still, relationships are the beauty of life—they are exchange, synergy and, most of all, the field for expressing love. They are where we can expand our capacity to be open and affectionate and also exercise our powers of withdrawing and detaching.

People enter relationships wishing for the same things—everyone wants to be acknowledged, loved and to feel happy. We expect cooperation and loyalty, and fear disappointment. Difficulties usually arise when both sides have unreasonable expectations or when there is attachment.

Attachment is a very subtle yet pervasive trait, and it usually hides insecurities or the demands of our egos. Unless we keep a balance through conscious awareness and realize the need to act as givers in relationships, there may come a point when we feel tired and sense that something is missing.

One of the reasons relationships have become so challenging is the lack of understanding that giving means receiving. Resentment arises when we stand on just one end, yet many people feel comfortable in this position. In this respect, there are a growing number of adults treating their parents as their lifelong support systems—emotional or material — not considering that there will come a time when the role of caretaker will have to be reversed.

In order to become whole, we need to realize that as much as we need love we also need freedom. There is growth and joy in togetherness only when our mental spaces are clean and clear and our creative energy is able to flow freely. No kind of commitment is worth our inner integrity and self-respect. For this we need the balance of detachment that comes with true love.

Being Connected
Exploring Relationships with God

At times we flow toward the Beloved like a dancing stream.
At times we are still water held in His pitcher.
At times we boil in a pot turning to vapor –
that is the job of the Beloved.

Jalal ad-Din Rumi – *A Garden Beyond Paradise*

Have you ever imagined how our relationships would be different if we entered them in a state of fulfillment? With nothing lacking internally, no hidden needs or expectations, yet wishing togetherness, sharing and receiving with joy and freedom?

Like all things in life, investing time and energy in spiritual development is a possibility. It is a choice which greatly affects and expands our worldview and brings positive changes to our existing relationships. As we move forward, we find ourselves happy both in the company of other fellow travelers as well as alone.

In fact, when you're developing internally there is a good chance that, from time to time, you might find yourself alone on the path. I don't mean the kind of loneliness that makes you deprived of companions, but the awareness that no one seems to be where you are at that moment. A little like the pupa which remains hidden while undergoing transformation, this is also a metamorphosis. What is deep within the self is not always easy to share. Maybe it is also not needed. This might have to do with learning to take the support of the One alone.

Spiritual knowledge teaches us to internalize our life experiences, which helps in creating movement in areas of stagnant emotional energy, throwing light on hidden parts of our souls. Old traits begin to resurface, and some of them may be of extraordinary quality, allowing us to realize things and perform in new ways. Others may not be so good, but they will become visible and will require our attention. The path of self-transformation has always been considered a journey of heroes, with symbolic imagery and myths created to celebrate it. There must be a reason why this is so.

Still, the more we develop our awareness, the more we find that there is in fact no other option. If we decide to postpone or avoid inner change, life's events will find a way of triggering it. External situations or relationships will end up putting things in motion, and this is not always nice, as it often involves some sort of suffering. Once again, it falls in our hands whether we want to learn to live and do things consciously, bit by bit, and get the chance to be empowered in the process.

Transformation means we learn to recreate ourselves and thereby come closer to the aspect of God as the Creator. We become his partners in the creation of a new consciousness. The Hopi people have a beautiful way of expressing this when they say that "we are the ones we have been waiting for."

We are certainly living in a world in turmoil where things happen fast, demanding adjustment and tolerance. Yet there is always a way of using whatever qualities we have to make the world a better place. This is not just a theory. Expanding our awareness through the light and love of God makes what appears to be impossible, possible.

This brings us to the sphere of spiritual experience. Most of us already have a personal picture of God, where he is seen as a specific deity or holy person, an all-pervasive energy or an Incorporeal Being.

Throughout history, it seems God was never too concerned about how we imagined or pictured him. But we have changed. We live in a time when the whole world is in need. He may continue to listen to us anyway, yet his response and capacity of reaching us is connected to the quality of our own inner feelings rather than to our ordinary thinking.

If we experience his presence and company in our lives, he can make us heirs to his qualities and powers. Whereas we make God our companion to be protected, he makes us his companions to protect the world.

Spiritual love fills the soul with pure, divine light, transforming consciousness on a deep level. The transmutation of our subconscious energies and the cleansing of our mind fields are effects of having a close relationship with the One Supreme. Yet for this to happen practically, we have to go beyond mere thinking. Philosophers and theologians have been reflecting on and discussing God—as a subject—for ages. Relationship implies a closer, mutual bond. The more we focus on an exchange based on feelings, the more we get to know him directly and have a chance to absorb his virtues and energy.

This is, after all, the relationship that reignites a spark in the soul, creating an enthusiasm and inner drive capable of inspiring new creativity. Divine love transforms us into channels for bringing a pure and subtle type of energy down into the Earth. Just like an alchemical process, it purifies and transforms a mind of iron into a mine of gold.

These transformative experiences have left amazing memorials and have inspired poets and thinkers for many generations. This is a relationship based on concentration and refinement of intellect as much as it is about the intensity and focus of our love.

In the next pages we will be exploring relationships that may give us a glimpse of the many faces of God, inspired by the teachings of a particular meditation school in India. I hope they inspire you in creating your own relationships. By entering the cosmic dimension that is connected with the One, we are able to reap the fruits of love and transcendent experiences.

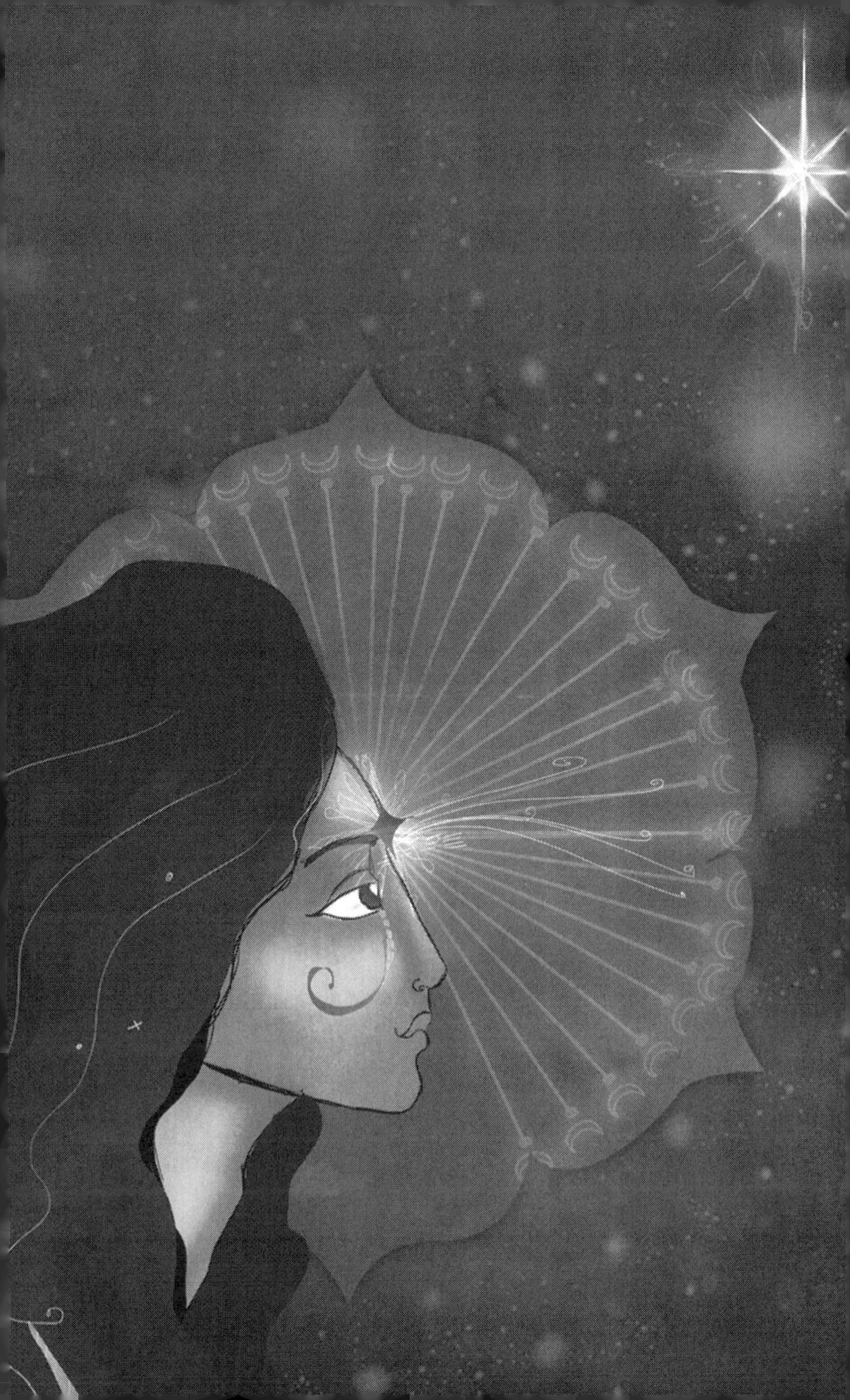

Bhagwan ke Yaadgar
God's Memorials

Parampita—The Father

The face that nurtures us and recognizes our innate goodness emerges through God's role of Parent. For it is the Father who has seen our life stories as well as our hard times, and therefore knows the reason children have grown weary and suspicious. He may adopt us if he is allowed to conquer our hearts rather than our reason or will power.

Maybe the most interesting feature of the Father is that he knows us better than we know ourselves. Because God's vision penetrates past, present and future, he always has the wide canvas of our many lives before him. That makes him capable of seeing things in perspective. He knows his children not only as they are at present, but how they were originally—as elevated and worthy of his love.

His vision falls on the soul alone, on the essence of our being—on our qualities and virtues rather than the present role we're playing. He remembers our highest stage; he has seen us fall and is watching our efforts in getting back on our feet again.

Whereas in our relationships, our sharing is usually conditioned by how we see and think of people, here we find someone with a completely different vision. As the Benefactor, God enters a relationship with the clear purpose of uplifting—of fathering and mothering, no matter the state one has reached. In a paternal relationship we feel protected and cared for, and we know we have the right to inherit treasures.

God's heart is of course merciful and beats only to alleviate suffering. From him there is never such a thing as a punishing thought, though he may advise and caution. Being filled with knowledge, he knows natural laws are responsible for correcting and eventually leveling things out. Yet the Father never loses hope or faith in his children.

People speak about "son showing father", or the child becoming the image of what is best in the parent. This is the relationship that produces such magic. It colors us with inner beauty and self-respect, creating great impact and influence on our emotional selves. To come close to the Father, we need recognition and deep realization.

There is endless praise for God's subtle activities, and as the Father he fulfills us deeply, knowing he has to give the return to those who have been calling on their Source of support.

Just as a physical father would sustain and give things to his children, the Spiritual Parent gives inner peace and love along with the inheritance of a new world. It is the Father who holds our hands and walks us through good and bad times, and who is there for us when we leave our present existence. He wishes his children to become knowledgeable and to be of service to others, so that eventually they become benefactors like him. He is the one common Parent that makes us into one world family.

Divya Mata
The Divine Mother

There are times we feel our lives are not what we expected. It is as if the external world does not match our innermost needs, or maybe we are not able to use our capacities and talents as we would have wished. It can be frustrating, especially when it occurs over a long period of time. This is often the cause behind depression, a lack of self-esteem and more severe illnesses.

We may think this is part of life, and accept that most people are suffering in one form or another from deprivation or loss. Economic crises and civil wars are currently triggering it collectively. It is difficult to talk about inner comfort with those who do not have a piece of bread. It is at such moments that we most need peace, love and acknowledgement.

There is no easy way to present God as the Mother, because words cannot convey her warmth and compassion or her attempts to save her children from suffering. When we're in any relationship with God, he is always present anyway, and there is never a cold shoulder from his side. In the form of Mother she is always there, welcoming us with the vibrations and vision of sustenance.

The Mother knows the causes behind life's events, for just like the Father, her vision penetrates time. Because she knows the invisible roots of situations, our failures or weaknesses do not color her vision but are seen rather as temporary and perfectly conquerable. Her task is to give unconditional support and help in our healing and transformation.

Maybe this is the reason why in India the divine feminine is symbolically shown in the form of powers—as *shaktis*. God as the Mother empowers us with her presence. There are a number of archetypes of goddesses who in fact personify spiritual attainments that can be received through meditation.

Knowing who we are and how we feel, God never underestimates our capability of overcoming obstacles and developing further. As the Divine Mother, she takes care of our internal needs through supportive vibrations, making sure we know how to access her power and put things right inside so that everything else can fall into place.

When I think of the many experiences of God as my parents, I remember a time when I was gently led through a very big situation. The motherly face became clearly manifested over that entire period and especially on one particular day when, sitting in a meditation room, I experienced God´s "tears" for me.

I know that at this point people may—justifiably—think this is all imagination or plain nonsense. Yet, though not physical, the kind of heartfelt empathy I received was almost tangible, and no words could express those feelings better. That experience formed an unbreakable bond between Mother and child. It also became an important lesson in my own understanding of God´s role, because those "tears" came after a very intense period of the Mother trying to save the child from sorrow. From then on, I learned to accept the fact that even though God is limitless in many ways, natural laws rule the show down here.

While the Father wishes for us to develop a higher form of reasoning so that we can succeed in our endeavors, the Mother is happy expressing her unbounded love and nurturing. She cannot bear to see the weaknesses of those she loves. This is the purity of her heart. Seeing the present world situation, her desire is for her children not to scatter their energies in useless circumstances and obstacles, but to learn how to make their present and future elevated.

Karankaravanhar
The One who Acts and Works through Others

Whatever god someone adores, it is I who answer their invocation.

Bhagavad Gita VII — 21, 22

Given his great subtlety, what would incorporeal God be able to do in a massively physical domain? Would his subtle senses really be able to work through others? This has been an ageless mystery.

If we look out in today's world to try to find clues of his presence, there is a great chance that we will become hopeless. Even reading these few pages may prove difficult to those who are out of touch. I'm aware that it is not easy or trendy to talk about God these days, unless it is in a religious context, or as a critical or science-related piece. It sometimes seems that people wish to continue to keep the One unfathomable, or simply to maintain him at a distance.

Still, we might sense, even if only by logic, that if such a being exists he must surely have his own ways and methods. After all, if God did not play a role in this "drama" of life, what would be the meaning of his existence?

There must definitely be ways through which he acts through others, even if indirectly, like a film director does. You might have experienced this yourself. Have you ever felt how sometimes, out of nowhere, a hand is extended in a time of need, or a word turns your mind in another direction and the light enters?

I don't mean to imply here that people do not play their own parts in expressing their ideas and free will. But it is different when you know that someone is acting rather as an instrument to share something precious or save you from something damaging. Quite often they are unaware of the message that they are holders.

Living beyond the physical world means God has no contact with negativities and vices, and that he does not have an ego that is directly related to the personas we've created for our interactions. Whatever action he inspires is related to something good, and his vibrations are powerful enough to produce waves of enthusiasm, creativity or happiness in us once we are tuned into them. This does not mean that all his work can be accomplished through simple inspiration.

In India, ancient scriptures talk about words of divine origin, such as *Shruti* (what is heard) and *Smriti* (what is remembered), and most religions believe speech is the means through which God's knowledge is manifested. Many spiritual paths also speak about a return of the Divine. The Bible calls it the time of Revelation, from the Greek "Apocalypse".

In fact, knowledge—or "the word"—is the basis of the creation myths of all peoples, which points to God's practical role as a teacher. The ancients believed that in the moment of transition, at the end of every cosmic cycle, the Supreme was bound to reveal himself. This would be when *Karankaravanhar* finally gets his act together. But would he then interfere?

God knows we live in a web of invisible bonds and ties even when we think we are free. He may open the eye of the intellect in those who wish to see a deeper, broader reality. He has to make us move forward; he wishes we would get rid of self-doubts and weaknesses in time to help others.

To cut through the web of negativity and waste that keeps pulling us down and binding us to the past, he is quick to show us another worldview, one that includes a brighter future. Instead of living entangled in obstacles, he wants us to create a new world for ourselves. Besides teachings, *Karankaravanhar* knows we need practical help as well as action.

To make use of material objects and relate to others without getting stuck or adding more bondages means we gradually learn to let go of things that trap us, things like "me" and "mine". Rather than running away from work or relationships, we learn the inner freedom that results from things done in a new way. We may experience, for example, that this is not "my possession or task", but rather something "I was given the opportunity to do". By becoming guardians of the things we use we are liberated from attaching our energy to objects. Our expectations are thereby minimized, and provided we have done the best we can, we are satisfied no matter the result.

God creates clever ways for us to put an end to attachment and suffering. If we are free and open to his influence, he can empower and inspire us to act, and much can be attained through this partnership. He knows that selfless and elevated actions create a beautiful karmic return, and in this way he is subtly pushing us into creating a new culture of sharing. As the song goes: "He does everything and then hides away…"

Param Shikshak — The Teacher
Spinning the discus of self-realization

One of the greatest treasures in life is a love of learning. It is openness to the new that brings richness and a sense of adventure to life, as well as the possibility of constantly renewing our inner resources. One is never too old, too tired, too outdated. Learning brings fulfillment, joy and new creativity. In relation to spiritual truths, it opens new territories with a unique depth and breadth of perspectives.

In ancient cultures, learning the secrets of spiritual reality was deemed sacred. The more the disciple proved worthy, the further he would be led into the teachings. One had to possess a good heart, humility, values and a good intellect to reach high levels. Understanding was not then only connected to absorbing information, but to developing inner integrity and wisdom. For this to be achieved, one needed method and structure.

This is the situation when it comes to a relationship with the Supreme Teacher. Having a vision that includes our past and future, and knowing the period of transition we are currently in, he teaches with a clear aim and objective in mind. He knows we are presently going through exams and that life will continue to test us. His work is to prepare us for the finals and make us capable of getting high marks.

What then would be the subjects that God would be able to teach us souls? He begins with interactive and experimental lessons that have to do with our capacity for understanding the core of life's reality. For that, the very first teaching is to disconnect oneself from the consciousness of the body and to experience the freedom of being a soul.

This is in fact not only the first teaching, but also the method for filling us with love, peace and inner powers. When this becomes firm, we develop further and begin to perceive and identify correspondences and experiment with the knowledge gained.

One of the benefits of becoming a spiritual student is that we start to see the world as a kind of playground of the lessons we need to assimilate. We can see why we are drawn to certain events, for they appear as having meaning. And we often find ourselves in a position of learning or teaching in any given situation, often both at the same time. This interconnection between inner and outer becomes a source of wonder, and we begin to see the magic that is life on this planet.

So, we learn not only what situations trigger in us, but also how to apply inner powers to overcome or transform them when necessary. The student wants to deal with the problems, for he knows that otherwise the same lesson will return later, clothed in another form. For this, God not only teaches us to act right and think positively; more than that, he gives us positive energy. The Teacher knows that there is benefit in everything that happens.

Patit Paavan
The Purifier and Healer of Hearts

I assume this is one of God's favorite roles. It is certainly one of the most pleasurable on the receiving end, so we might well have a look at what purification really involves.

God's energy, being so rarefied, can only act on our higher levels, which means he can reach our most subtle faculties, not the physical body. And this can only happen when we are open and willing to receive his light. His penetrating energy has a purifying effect, bringing clarity, awareness and positively influencing our negative traits, such as anger.

Anger is one of the most serious and spread out diseases of our time. It causes wars and illnesses as it erupts, shattering everything in its way, destroying relationships and creating obstacles to self-development.

Everyone has one or another way of manifesting anger. This is an old enemy, and therefore it still rules some part of our being. Even when you meditate and find your balance, there is a good chance something may come up, cause a stir and try to pull you back to a position of reacting.

The question is, how should we then respond? Some people think that negative emotions need to be expressed or at least vented so that calmness can then settle in. Spiritually we understand that there is only loss in both the feeling and expression of any negativity.

Anger is one of those traits that need to be attended to. Even though a forceful burst may at times appear externally as a manifestation of strength, anger is actually a weakness. It is not only the antithesis of love; its turbulent and often autonomous expression is experienced by the mind as a drain, one that robs the soul of its peace and self-esteem. Our sense of dignity is gradually undermined by anger and other vicious habits.

Only when we begin to establish honest contact with the roots of anger can we begin to tame it. When something negative becomes conscious, it stops to dominate us with the same force. This might require effort and focus, and it might take time. We might also be surprised to observe how this erupting energy can emerge through different triggers.

It is therefore helpful to become aware of the "quality" and frequency of every negative trait we carry and express. This might not be so obvious, for their causes are frequently rooted in the past. Still, it is important that we realize that negative responses have a subtle way of undermining our efforts toward goodness and wholeness. Try to see what your unconscious is demanding when anger shows its head. Is it connected, for example, with a feeling of frustration, envy, despondency or unfulfilled expectation? The list of causes is immense, and responses will vary according to self-awareness.

Ego usually plays a big role in negative responses. Sometimes it emerges clothed as revolt or as a manifestation of powerlessness. It takes maturity and inner strength to accept the twists of life and to see reality as it is, without inner complaints.

It is important that we do not repress our feelings or feel ashamed when getting in contact with our shadows, that we do it with a feeling of care, knowing that the soul deserves love and respect, that it has gone through so much already. There are parts of us that need to be healed, and they may manifest in the way we react to situations. Whatever is balanced and virtuous in the self will not be expressed in the same manner, for qualities and virtues have a way of simply flowing through life. So, the manifestation of our negative side is the only way we have to understand our unconscious baggage and then to gauge the "amount and frequency" of the treatment.

The cure involves unconditional love and deep silence, and it is here where the Purifier comes in.

There is nothing even remotely similar to the effect of God's energy on our being when it comes to dissipating negativity. Yet it is up to us to recognize that we do have within us things we don't need—vices that burden the mind and restrict one's freedom and happiness. We can be sure he will play his part to its conclusion once we maintain a connection and keep making our efforts.

The Purifier is a unique healer who can soothe and transform hearts and minds. The treatment is based on self-knowledge together with frequent doses of meditation and a firm determination not to give up. Its duration is a lifetime, for there will always be new situations to explore and perfect. Patience and tolerance with yourself and others will be necessary complements. God's powerful love and light and our merciful responses to our shadows will definitely bring a radical change to the deepest and neediest parts of our souls.

Prem ka Sagar
The Ocean of Love and Cosmic Experiences

Love has nothing to do with the five senses and the six directions: its goal is only to experience the attraction exerted by the Beloved.
Afterwards, perhaps, permission will come from God: the secrets that ought to be told will be told with an eloquence nearer to the understanding than these subtle confusing allusions.
The secret is partner with none but the knower of the secret: in the skeptic's ear the secret is no secret at all.

Jalal Al-Din Rumi – *Mathnawi III*

If you practice meditation, you have probably wondered what could make one into a "recipient" of the transcendent. Are "out of this world" experiences something anyone can aim for, or are they only a privilege of sages and saints?

The answer once again seems to lie in a loving intellect. Even though experiences may at times come spontaneously, as gifts, I've observed how they usually come as a result of focused contemplation over a period of time. As in preparing the soil before planting, it is deep reflection that leads us to realizations. The intellect needs to be clear in order to receive and perceive connections, for thoughts have a way of emerging from the subconscious before they begin to form a picture and become fully formed.

Realizations can often trigger deep experiences in meditation. These don´t necessarily come in the form of thunder and visions, but may touch something deep within, bringing out a sort of magical transformation in the self. It is like, when after a few moments of connection you suddenly feel so sweet, so patient...

Coming across yogis who managed the art of balancing their worldly lives with the spiritual was important at the beginning of my practice. I could see them going around their businesses and families and at the same time opening up and developing inside. I was impressed that they were not afraid of sacrificing things that most people think are necessary in life. They decided to live in discipline in order to have elevated experiences. This was almost tangible in its effect of making the atmosphere clean and charged with energy. An oasis of light met those who came to meditate in their company. It felt as if they became clear vessels for God´s might and love to come through.

This has come to deepen my way of understanding spiritual life. More than beautiful words, a nice setting or inspiring music, it is cleanliness in the soul that seems to open a space for divine love to enter and stay safe in the heart.

This exercise of the heart has to be continuous to be effective, and for this reason it is a challenge. Yet because the time is right, there is also constant help if one is willing to accept it. In this age of change, the One who lives beyond is interested in leading us back to our original and perfect nature. And to accomplish this task, he has to give us spiritual experiences. So he will find one or another way of doing it, once we are ready.

To become ready we have to open up to that thing we have learned to call faith. Faith is not only close to spiritual love, but also a beautiful way to fortify the mind before entering the doors of altered perception safely. When one has that sensibility, along with the support of discipline, taking the mind to the highest region is a possibility. This is where the meeting of hearts takes place.

The experiences we have in meditation are, however, different from what is known as "astral traveling", which usually happens in the etheric fields around us. In fact, this "unfolding" of the astral body can also happen during sleep, and most of what we experience in this state is connected to our past and emotional selves.

God's realm is the highest destiny; it is far beyond. Because he does not experience things through the physical senses like we do, he wants us to experience his pure dimension of light. He wants us to feel love and bliss as he does. Try connecting to his loving energy, and the more you feel, the more you will be pulled up closer.

Divya Kratavya
The Divine Activity of the Creator

I have seen many kinds of trees growing from the Earth, but who has ever seen the birth of Paradise?

Jalal Al-Din Rumi – *A World Inside this World*

Over the last few decades, debates between creationists and Darwinists have turned the subject of creation into a controversy. I once imagined God lending an ear to their discussions, as a Father would with his children—with a smile on his face. After all, he might have thought, at least they are talking about something meaningful.

As with other reflections, here I can also go as far as sharing a few insights. However, we might be in agreement on this one aspect—the One we call the Supreme is a conscious Being who has been in contact with many of us throughout history.

If we consider his nature as non-physical or incorporeal, we may also realize that whatever he creates is necessarily also on that invisible, non-material level. Thanks to quantum physics, we now know that on this level there is impermanence or constant change.

Many yogis are presently experiencing how God's energy is capable of influencing the deepest levels of human consciousness. Because these experiences happen through our intellect and mind fields, they generate ripples of renewal that affect the subtle elements of nature. We become channels for new energy to enter the planet. Creation of new consciousness and subtle transformation are being triggered by this process.

We know that nature operates in cycles. It is not only our daily lives that are moved by cycles of light and darkness, by seasons moved by the rotation of the Earth or civilizations that rise and fall. On a larger scale, our story is eternal and recurring, as the soul travels through an ongoing cycle of births and rebirths. Life is an interplay between the Supreme, human souls and the energies of matter.

God's vision, being of a spiritual nature, is never constrained by limitations. Within the cyclic perspective of time, his role as Creator has more to do with recreating order out of chaos. And he does that by empowering and leading us through lessons that gradually take us back to our true selves. It is through his light and wisdom that one becomes "enlightened".

As the Creator, his task is connected with us humans, with his pure vibrations reaching down here, affecting and transforming us. Through soul connection, he purifies and regenerates our energy, inspiring those actions that will turn into good fruits. His teachings are about the greatest donation being qualities and virtues and how such actions will surely bring a new future.

In this respect, we learn that creation is not based on thoughts, meditation or will power alone—though these are the foundation. For a new world we need selfless actions, the openness of being of service to others. The coming age will be governed by true spiritual radiance, and it is our individual inner light that will determine our birth in the world to follow.

Gyan ka Surya
The Sun of Knowledge

You shine beautifully on the horizon of heaven;
You, living Sun; Bestower of life!
You fill every land with your beauty;
You are gracious, you are great; gleaming and high over every land;
Your rays embrace all you have created
Though you are far, your light touches the earth;
Men see you, but know not your ways.
How manifold are your works: they are hidden from our sight.
Oh unique God, no other is like you.

Pharaoh Akhenaten – *Excerpts from Hymn to Aten*

The image of a system of multiple stars revolving around a sun is suggestive enough to have this planet as a symbol for the One who shines supreme among us living stars. The fact that there could not be life as we know it without the existence, light and warmth produced by this planet adds to the picture of us basking in the rays of a corresponding spiritual Sun in whose subtle magnetism we souls orbit.

The sun as a symbol has inspired thinkers across the ages and was the basis for a spiritual revolution in antiquity during the reign of pharaoh Akhenaten—"the living spirit of Aten".

His reformation broke with tradition in a time when all kingdoms were ruled and protected by a number of deities zealously guarded by powerful temple priests. The land of Khemet—today's Egypt—had been a theocracy for many generations, and spiritual development was at the core of its foundation. Yet dogma and lust for power was already corrupting and degrading this extraordinary civilization.

That seems to have been the backdrop for the young and learned pharaoh to carry on a radical reform—one that probably cost him his life. He must have felt deeply inspired to take the risk of officially changing the old system of rituals and priesthood—in favor of a single Light God. He might have wished to inspire his people by reviving old religious feelings. And he began by doing it himself—by dedicating part of his time to meditation and devotional composition. Akhenaten's period also left a legacy of change in diplomacy, in the arts and culture, and this is the first time we get such a close and colorful glimpse of life in the court—of their warm family relationships, daily activities, sports and spiritual rituals.

"Praise to you Aten—Lord of rays—who rises on the horizon day by day! Shine with your beams of light upon the faces of those who speak the truth."

There are a number of speculations around the life and fate of this sage-king and his famous queen Nefertiti, who by all accounts seems to have been an equal partner in the establishment of the new religion. In order to accomplish their bold project, they built a new capital from scratch—the city of Akhet-Aten.

What have reached us from this period are fragmented accounts and chance discoveries, like the bust of Nefertiti. We know they must have paid a high price for manifesting their spiritual beliefs, for their revolutionary changes triggered violent reactions which wrote off their names from subsequent royal genealogy. Akhenaten became the heretic king, lost from history until modern times.

Yet it is from the beautiful carvings, frescoes and poems in the mountain caves of his vanished city that we get to see their artwork and have a glimpse into the pharaoh's mind. Some scholars like to refer to Akhenaten as the first individual in history, as well as the first monotheist.

God as the Sun of Knowledge evokes in us this same ancient belief that life keeps renewing itself and that this happens through knowledge of truth. In all myths of creation there are allusions to a primeval age when truth is revealed and new beginnings that recur when the time is ripe.

We may take this as more than just a metaphor. When it comes to spiritual enlightenment, the role of study and integrity can never be overemphasized. The attitude of constant learning helps us to maintain inner stability, contentment and connection with truth. And when outside circumstances seem to conspire to limit us on every level, we can always count on resources of wisdom to take us across.

Spiritual knowledge empowers the soul and becomes the basis of qualities and values that keep the inner light always burning.

Bholanath
The Lord of Innocence

*Stand for a moment and look at a desert of thorns—
it becomes a flowery garden. See that boulder on the
ground? It moves, and a mine of rubies appears.
Wash your hands and face in the waters of this place—
the cooks have prepared a great feast!*

Jalal Al-Din Rumi – *A World Inside this World*

Our personality traits, memories and knowledge come from life experiences. Both mind and intellect work based on these events, in a conscious or unconscious manner. Considering that God's mind and intellect never get involved with relationships and physical things as we do—through performing actions and reaping their fruits; by acting and reacting—we can see why he is able to remain untouched in the lightness of his Being. Maybe this is the secret behind all the positivity we find in his role as *Bholanath*.

Here we have the games of magic and play, of wonders of past and future shown to us in a childlike fashion. And maybe because of our own innocence, we are at times able to see and feel things not as they are, but while in the process of becoming.

This is the face that appears when God's spontaneity comes into play, inspiring and bringing out a sense of easiness and a carefree attitude in us. We get colored by his enthusiasm, sweetness and tangible closeness, and our features change. They become angelic. People might even be able to see our simplicity, but they will never guess our depth.

It is interesting to observe how "worldly intelligence" works when you start to value things from a spiritual perspective. Not only because it rules today's world—where it is often equated with "having your way and getting what you want"— but also because of the overrated value given to external success and material gains.

As we have seen, spiritual intelligence works in different ways. It makes connections where no one can see them, improves the ability to predict or prevent and develops the capability of using love and mercy in the expression of will. In his Innocent role, God is the master of pure feelings.

This title also has a connection with the openness with which God reaches us and how he does not condition his presence and giving by anything we have said or done. He has the key to the "treasure store" and everyone is welcome to take whatever he or she needs. In the eyes of *Bholanath* there are no sinners, no defamers—just children in need of company and support.

As a loyal friend, he not only walks the extra mile but he remains with us until we´ve reached our destination. The company of the Innocent Lord is always entertaining and light; it guides us across situations so that we reach our destination filled with treasures. That is, provided we walk with honesty, for *Bholanath* does not respond to external cleverness. His love is able to reach those with a pure heart.

Nyara – The Unique and Detached Observer

We moderns are faced with the need of rediscovering the life of the spirit; we must experience it anew for ourselves. It is the only way in which to break the spell that binds us to the cycle of biological events. The wheel of history must not be turned back, and man's advance toward a spiritual life must not be denied...

He must even be able to admit that the ego is sick for the very reason that it is cut off from the whole, and has lost its connection not only with mankind but with the spirit.

Carl Jung – *Freud and Psychoanalysis*

Some cultures are more open to things of the spirit than others. I myself have seen how, in some countries, one has to take great care when sharing spiritual experiences, and even more when talking about God.

While for many this is a totally irrelevant subject, and others find it too pretentious, those with crystalized concepts find no point in listening to anything that may go against their established views. This is a sensitive issue.

So, even though for the indifferent it doesn't really matter and it might not be wise to talk to the converted, the true seeker is always open to experimenting.

I like to imagine the perspective of the One living beyond when he is watching his indifferent, opinionated and seeking children. This is when his face of the Detached Observer is most clear to me. For could there be a better attitude than being constantly loving and yet totally detached?

God's capacity for non-judgment and emotional detachment is certainly something we can aspire to; these traits can come handy in many circumstances. But we had better be clear—detachment has nothing to do with coldness or insensitivity. In fact, it's the perfect balance for love. In a state of detachment there is stability, self-respect and inner power, and one is not affected by the oscillations or projections of others.

Paradoxically, this is also a quality that few of us have sympathy for. A lot of denial and disappointment regarding God's existence, as well as his perspective and means of operating, seems to be related to a lack of recognition of this virtue.

God knows too well—not from books, scriptures or theories, but from direct observance—how, at any given moment, the law of karma keeps unfolding and playing things out down here, creating ripples in our personal lives and world events. Whether it is pleasure or pain, there is no action without reaction, no results without effort.

His role as Detached Observer is therefore an aspect of his wisdom. Even the Supreme is bound by the laws that rule and regulate life on this planet. This means that even if he wanted to save someone from falling—and he sometimes does do so—that soul would continue to be guided by its own free will and would sooner or later meet its destiny. In specific cases, God´s energy may heal the sick, yet the person might want to continue with an unhealthy attitude. When it comes to spiritual reality, things are not so evident and simple; hidden aspects have to be taken into account.

Ultimately, it requires all our capacity, will power and determination to come out and get liberated from the karmic web we´ve created for ourselves. Personal responsibility is one of the first realizations in the process of spiritual awakening.

It is by knowing that everything will be automatically sorted out by natural means that God, as a Detached Observer, can remain always unaffected and without any worries. He is able to see benefit where we see only difficulty, for he knows that it is by working hard that we can reshape our personality and regain our strength and inner truth.

Likewise, only by being carefree and detached are we able to judge and gauge precisely and in this way become an instrument of help in the lives of others.

SatGuru
The True Guide

Where do you stand behind them all, my lover, hiding yourself in the shadows? They push you and pass you by on the dusty road, taking you for nothing. I wait here weary hours spreading my offerings for you, while passers-by come and take my flowers, one by one, and my basket is nearly empty. The morning time is past, and the noon. In the shade of evening my eyes are drowsy with sleep. Men going home glance at me and smile, and fill me with shame. I sit like a beggar, drawing my skirt over my face, and when they ask me, what it is I want, I drop my eyes and answer them not. Oh, how, indeed, could I tell them that for you I wait, and that you have promised to come.

Rabindranath Tagore – *Gitanjali*

There is an ancient feeling here, a sense of having been together throughout the ages and again becoming close at the moment of transition. As the guide, God has the responsibility of leading us to the right destination, but not before showing us how the return journey is part of the play. He knows that the tip that is just needed will soon cause the wheel to turn and events to take a new course. The Satguru has been remembered as leading a celestial procession across the sky in a cosmic journey of return.

In the company of the Guide, a sense of depth and sacredness emerges, a disposition based on love for truth rather than blind worship. People bow down at the feet of gurus, but this One is incorporeal and egoless. Still, spontaneous feelings of devotion may arise, like those we have for the Beloved. After all, this is the One we could really place higher, yet the only altar he can stand upon is the Universe.

God in this role gives us a picture of infinite time and space. He sows in us the eternal seeds of righteousness and depth, which ultimately work in disentangling past bondages and creating a new future. True and trustworthy, he treats us with deep respect and unlimited benevolence.

It is clear that the Guide is not after worshippers but knows who his true followers are; after all, his task is to create masters self-sovereigns. That we may find God associated with royalty might seem rather unusual, not least because monarchy has often been related to unfair and undemocratic values. This has, however, not always been the case. In ancient cultures, due to knowledge of self and karmic law, souls born into ruling families were regarded as highly special and looked upon as benefactors.

As we come to understand how spiritual development leads us to independence and how from this position we may be of service to others, the image of the king may acquire a different meaning. What is *swaraj*—self-rule—but the original state of the soul when complete with all qualities and internally empowered. Here we have the archetype of sovereignty taking shape in real life.

This is another beautiful aspect of a relationship with the Supreme. His energy of love, dignity and peace fills and colors us in such a way that the soul's inner purity resurfaces out of this alchemy in a quiet and unassuming way. Our vibrations and characters are transformed, and in the process we generate energy that is bound to give birth to a new way of living.

God as the guru does not need rituals, mantras or admiration. He has no image and does not expect to be adored, yet he loves to receive our love. When connecting with the Highest Guide, a sense of holiness hangs in the atmosphere. We are touched by transcendent reality. The true guide takes us back home.

Sarvashaktiman
The Almighty Authority

The aim of all human existence is the return to the source. This is the message of all initiatic teachings. We are here, according to these teachings, to work to regain that higher state of consciousness that is our birthright. If we fail to fulfill this responsibility, then our biological survival is of no particular importance and our preoccupation with utility meaningless. Whatever contributes to the acquisition of consciousness is useful.

John Anthony West – *Serpent in the Sky*

This is the closest we can get to true power and the personality that emerges from inner truth, centeredness and detachment.

God's presence is magnetic, majestic—it emanates and pulls with gentle force. It is strength that cannot be measured by our standards, which are always based on the limitations of physical senses. In order to receive God's power, you first have to become still. Your mind needs to be quiet, your intellect connected.

You may well ponder—why would God be interested in empowering us? I´d rather think that he knows which qualities and powers can be used for the right purposes, and can inspire many to live and act according to *dharmic*—natural—laws.

In this connection we find memorials of spiritual warriors in many places. In ancient India, they speak of heroes who "battled with Maya"—the illusions created by mental habits which are still the root cause of so much sorrow and loss.

In our culture, most people consider power to be something visible, manifested in people´s positions, attitudes and behaviors. Try to imagine how it feels when strength arises from the depth of your soul. In meditation you may picture yourself as being internally free, stable in soul consciousness. Let your thoughts focus on God´s light; be receptive to his vibrations. Trust that his current will pull you closer and lead you into quietness, then gradually into silence. You have gone beyond the senses, you feel full rather than empty. This is the highest stage, the greatest experience of power one can possibly have.

Such experiences never leave you the same. When you return, things have changed, you have acquired something; you have gained energy, enthusiasm. They also reawaken inner powers from within the subconscious mind. And these come just in time for life in this troubled age.

Connecting is the method for regaining inner powers, to attain qualities like tolerance, concentration, the capacity of letting go, depth in discriminating and judging, a new courage and sense of cooperation…

Here again, it all comes back to us—to be empowered and exercise authority in a new way. It is as if nothing is in the hands of God alone. The Almighty says, remember me and you will receive power—but use it wisely.

Dharamraj
The Lord of Righteousness
"Do not give sorrow, do not take sorrow..."

This is a known face, especially in the more traditional religions where a Supreme Judge is remembered and even feared at times. While there may be a "serious" side to God's personality, once we really understand natural laws, it becomes clear that we only go through things we have created. There is in fact not even any need for him to know what we've been doing. So where has this fearful image of a punishing God calling us into account emerged from?

I like to connect this title with another aspect of God, which is that of *Mahakal*—"the Death of all deaths"—for it is here that I get a glimpse of his unlimited vision. Nobody else can know us so deeply or see us as we truly are—as immortal, eternal souls.

As we approach existence from the perspective of death—of being away from the physical vehicle—all fears and prejudices that exist in the limited understanding of corporeal life are disintegrated. For in this stage we experience the fact that there is no such thing as death, even though there is suffering. And this is what the Lord of Righteousness wants us to understand and conquer.

Changing consciousness depends of course on our capacity for understanding, will and involvement. To understand that suffering results from the slightest detour from righteousness makes us re-evaluate things. Sorrow may take many forms—it may just be a mild sadness, or it may be shocking—but it still throws life out of balance.

This face of God seems to work like a clear mirror of perfection, which can reflect back our weaknesses simply by being there. We feel safe enough to measure ourselves against the Lord of Righteousness and share with him what we´ve done. I´m sure this is an important aspect, one that might be needed for our education.

It is human nature to overlook things we don´t like, as when we think, for example, "everything is relative anyway" or "it all depends on our intentions", etc. Yet nothing is relative when it comes to reaping the fruits of action. There is a very definite, unambiguous difference between positive and negative qualities and what they generate in life.

Besides, we have to consider that we often discriminate and judge things from a limited perspective. What may appear outwardly hard or difficult may actually be an opportunity for us to adjust and develop new strength.

The soul plays different roles from life to life, experiencing changes in its mental capacities, genre, wealth, physical strength, quality of relationships, etc. Life is like that because we need to learn our lessons and be absolved of past mistakes. The Lord of Righteousness never forgets that his children need learning in order to develop and become free again.

Paras — The Alchemist
*Dancing over fire–knowing things
will shake, I become unmovable*

*True words aren't eloquent, eloquent words aren't true.
Wise men don't need to prove their point, men who need to prove their point aren't wise.
The wise man does his job and then stops.
He understands that the Universe is forever out of control, and that trying to dominate events goes against the current of the Way. Because he believes in himself, he doesn't try to convince others. Because he is content with himself, he doesn't need others' approval. Because he accepts himself, the whole world accepts him.*

Lao Tzu – *Tao Te Ching*

Alchemy was born as a path of transmutation of consciousness, where the soul was viewed as the *prima materia* or the focus of the work. By making use of a symbolic "philosopher's stone"—a wise intellect—the alchemist believed himself able to reawaken his dormant inner powers. This was in fact a beautiful metaphor for the process of inner transformation.

All ancient teachings regarded self-realization as the basis of true civilization. In practice this meant developing mental and intellectual powers like will, concentration, intuition, creativity, a set of qualities and values, etc. These attempts at returning to a pristine state of consciousness considered perfection an achievable goal. Alchemy pointed to the idea that, spiritually, our lowest nature—lead—could be transformed into gold.

Most esoteric teachings are actually symbolist methods which have a common origin. They are based on the transmutation of the soul when in contact with the most subtle and yet enormously powerful energy of the Supreme. Many such archetypes and memorials are connected with the cyclic perspective of time, where an "iron-aged" world is believed to disappear before the birth of a new golden age. In this respect, alchemy does not measure words when describing the stages of purification of the human soul before reaching completion.

In fact, ancient traditions valued aspects of mental energy that we've ended up forgetting. As we continue to live and operate from a limited state of awareness, we keep seeing things as disconnected and random. Most people think this is how life is anyway. From this angle, physical things appear if not the same, then pretty much so. After all, everyone has a body with a head, two arms and legs, and so on.

From an energetic point of view we are, however, completely different. Ask someone who has the ability known as clairvoyance to tell you how people appear to them in terms of energy and light. Everyone is unique when it comes to one´s aura, one´s orb of light or lack of it. On this level, nothing can remain hidden.

In this sense, we may think of God´s light as the actual philosopher's stone, capable of melting the lead of our deep-rooted, negative traits, provided we are willing to do "the work".

The *magnum opus*—the great work of the alchemist—was usually performed with great secrecy in the darkness of the night. Similarly, it is in the darkest hour of the soul that we sit in silence and work on our inner transformation.

There is no greater task than this, not only for our selves but for the sake of our world. We can be sure that the Universe rewards us with blessings as we connect with the One. This is the great incognito effort.

Bhagwan ka Avataran
The Incarnation of God

"Leave your throne of the sky and come down to earth."
Indian devotional song

Whenever we concentrate deeply and intensely in meditation or prayer, we naturally detach and move upward. It feels as if the weight or density of the body gets loosened by the power of the vehicle of the mind. Our subtle awareness may then unfold and travel to subtler dimensions where transcendental experiences take place. We ascend—even if only for a temporary period. The more we practice, the easier it gets, for our mind fields are strengthened by the light and power received in the spiritual encounter. We can have such experiences when in the state we may call "the bodiless stage".

At this point there are no more distractions, the soul is totally involved in and merged with the experience, and the mind is filled with peace and strength. There is nothing but silence and ethereal light, which is clearly visible when our eyes are slightly opened. This is the closest to experience the incorporeal state while in the body. We ascend in soul consciousness to have a meeting with the Supreme and return having absorbed some of his qualities and powers.

Yet, the world awaits God's descent. At the beginning of the twenty-first century, despite all the wonders of modern life and science, people still long for divine intervention to save us from chaos.

All religious traditions talk about a return of the Divine. While many have been seeking and longing for God, others believe a Messiah or a Buddha will appear before the end times. The Bible suggests he will come incognito, "like a thief in the night". So we may well ponder: how would he make his presence felt, and how would he possibly be recognized—and accepted—by souls from all religions, from all corners of the earth?

Many people experience contact with this most subtle of Beings through meditation or prayer. No thunder and fireworks here—God has no need for a big show. His vibrations are those of stillness and deep silence, and we tune in to be able to catch them. So try to think of a reason God would "leave his throne in the sky" and come down here other than being needed and for the sake of helping us.

In India there is the tradition of the *Avatar* or "incarnation". A few stories suggest that the highest Being has to make use of a human chariot—a body—in order to manifest himself and give knowledge. The chariot is also known as *bhagirath*—the fortunate instrument.

Another memorial is the symbolic dialogue between the Supreme and the human soul, which is the core of India's most beloved scripture, the Bhagavad Gita—"the Song of God". Its core teachings beautifully depict the many doubts and trials one faces when on the path of self-transformation.

In this epic, one of God's tasks is to help the heroes in their efforts to tame their horses, graphically shown as the five senses of sight, touch, hearing, taste and smell. He personally instructs the prince-warrior on how to go beyond physical perception in order to connect with the Divine.

Learning how to transcend our identification with matter and physical things and to be loving and detached in relationships is the basis of the story. Detachment from one's ego and outdated conceptions is shown as the path for conquering the mind, which is also the last stage of the teachings. They repeatedly point to *Manmanabhav*—or keeping the mind focused on the One—as the way to receive spiritual support and strength.

The need for transcending our limited selves and renouncing desires in order to attain spiritual treasures is the underlying theme of religious literature. It seems we have come full circle and reached the point where looking at the self is no longer just an option.

Maybe the *Avatar* aspect of God will be revealed by those who have been touched by his light and changed through his knowledge and power. He may then become visible through the faces and actions of ordinary people who have engaged in the extraordinary feat of taming their wild horses. God's light is capable of transforming humans into angels.

Nirakari – The Incorporeal

I seem to have loved you in numberless forms, numberless times, in life after life, in age after age, forever. Whenever I hear old chronicles of love, its age-old pain, its ancient tale of being apart or together, as I stare on and on into the past, in the end you emerge clad in the light of a pole-star, piercing the darkness of time: You become an image of what is remembered forever.

Rabindranath Tagore – *Unending Love—Gitanjali*

Duality and non-duality are diametrically opposed concepts which have been the subject of philosophical discussions for ages. They are based on reflections and conjectures on the true nature of the Supreme.

In duality, the highest Being is considered to exist separated from us humans and the natural world. He is believed to have consciousness, intelligence and traits of his own, and of being capable of revealing himself whenever and to whomever he chooses.

In non-duality—also known as *Advaita*—God is believed to be immanent in Creation. That means he would be present on an invisible level, not only in our highest selves but also in the natural world. He would be sort of hidden inside everything, in humans and animals, pebbles and stones.

For some reason this last approach has gained a lot of popularity among scholars and spiritual teachers, and it is not difficult to guess why. In fact, when in close contact with God´s light, one does feel unity, as if he is temporarily part of that same radiant orb that reaches the soul.

When we are lost in the remembrance of someone close to our hearts, a similar feeling takes place as we pull and merge that image and vibration within ourselves. Therefore, the feeling of closeness produced by "omnipresence" is as legitimate as that of "the One I´ve been looking for is out there, ready to meet me". Feelings and reality are, however, different things.

Just like in science, where so much continues to be unveiled and clarified, this would require similar attention and research. We would need to go beyond the limits of feeling in order to verify what is in fact true by direct experience. Even if we only consider logic and the understanding of natural laws, we may realize that the concept of omnipresence implies that God would also be subject to the laws of rise and decay, to loss of energy (entropy).

Any soul in this condition could not be experienced as an eternal Source of strength and support.

Here the knowledge of the cyclic perspective of time and karmic dynamics is of great importance. Once we enter the cycle of birth and rebirth, there is no way we can be immune to the effects of our actions, even on a mental level. If God could truly be intertwined with us humans and matter, it would be impossible for his energy and wisdom to come to our rescue on any level. That is but one aspect.

This is a subject that deserves a much closer look and many more pages. The fact that non-duality has gained so much ground with meditators has made close encounters or deep yogic experiences more difficult to attain. The concept of union—which is the very meaning of yoga—presupposes two parties and was born out of the experience of spiritual connection between the human soul and the Supreme.

It is clear that we are in no need of more rhetoric and philosophy at this point. What really matters is having experiences that are fulfilling and transformative. It is therefore up to us to test the two approaches and find out which one works.

Piyu — The Beloved

The time has come to turn your heart
into a temple of fire.
Your essence is gold hidden in dust.
To reveal its splendor you need to burn in the fire of love.

Jalal ad-Din Rumi – *Whispers of the Beloved*

There is a level of closeness like no other here, an intensity created by depth, surrender and loyalty of the heart. When we are in love with the Beloved, our psychic energy expands out far and wide in waves of joy and bright light that reach high. Life then seems to render itself to us, bringing surprises and gifts in the most unexpected ways. This may happen because we become channels of the purest love.

When love is so deeply felt, it is returned by God's intensity and potency in its most radiant form. This is, after all, not just another love relationship. No wonder mystics and sages have been praising it for ages, for it feels as if we are tuning into the heartbeat of the Universe.

As we become merged in divine love, our feelings create ripples that touch people's lives and create changes in them. We become witness to the subtle transformations in others as their best qualities get a chance to be expressed and acknowledged. This happens because they are being accepted and subtly sustained by genuine affection. Our own difficulties get sorted out, for we seem to be able to accommodate and adjust to things so much more easily. The vibrations of love do all the work.

What would then be the secret for us to be able to sit on God's heart throne? Maybe there is no secret, but there is definitely something like a password. As I remember the mystics, it is as if their minds had wings that allowed them to fly high and become totally merged in the One alone. Their focus was not only born out of love, but from detachment from whatever was limited and small in life.

Yogis know from experience that the more one goes beyond ego and temporary desires, the easier it is to be stable in the eternal soul. Identification with the limited self is such that it appears in connection with most physical and mental aspects that we tend to associate with too closely. Even when on a spiritual journey, ego finds a way to sneak in, subtly pushing its way into things like recognition, position, experience, etc. However, the more we are able to renounce, the more the unlimited can make a home in our hearts. The Beloved needs that space.

Such love can then take the form of fire. Everything is destroyed in a fire—all bondages are finished in the fire of intense love. No weaknesses or doubts can remain when we are merged in divine love.

This is something we can learn, and yet it belongs to us already. The more the soul becomes detached and lost in the love of the Beloved, the more the mind can catch God's vibrations and radiant beauty. Tasting it just once seems to do the trick—we get hooked. Nothing in this world can compare to it.

Cause and Effect

Empty yourself.
Let your mind rest.
All the things of the world rise and fall
While the soul catches their return.
Everything grows and flourishes,
then returns to the source of stillness.
This is unchanging, eternal.
To know this constancy is insight.
To know this constancy frees the mind.
A free mind brings an open heart.
Open-hearted, you will act royally.
Being royal you attain the divine.
Being divine you will be your true self,
Your eternal self.
The body dies, the soul will never pass away.

Lao Tzu – *Tao Te Ching*

The Sanskrit word "karma" stands for action and its result, for the fact that whatever we sow in our lives returns to us sooner or later. It is a vast and deep concept from which we continue to learn new lessons. For the spiritual student, an understanding of personal karma may work as a motivator to deepen awareness and embody positive attitudes. The more we internalize, the more we realize the extent to which we are moved by deep-rooted habits and how we often think and act in an automatic way. At times we may be lacking long-term vision or just find ourselves too tired or busy to care. Our *dharma*—the knowledge and experience of the spirit—must run deep for our values and direction to remain right.

There is no more important and yet challenging teaching than that of righteous action. The philosophy is straight and simple—you get what you give. Still, interpretations are full of nuances. This happens because our values and understanding of aspects like right and wrong vary according to our consciousness, culture, context and time period. But relativism is not applicable to the law of karma, for as with some physical laws, there is an exact universal constant operating in its spiritual counterpart.

It might have been easier for us to assimilate such things if spiritual teachings were with us from an early age. This would make a difference in the way we envision life and save the world a lot of trouble.

The tricky thing about karma is that it stretches beyond the limits of a lifetime and therefore is one of those things that cannot be empirically seen or proved. Such a notion is not easily acceptable for most people living in this age of material reasoning and quick fixes.

Besides, this is the kind of knowledge that historically has been kept away from the masses, remaining a privilege of esoteric initiates. Many mystical schools were structured around what was left from ancient teachings related to soul realization and its connection with the natural world. In certain time periods, such as the medieval Inquisition, it was a risk to merely ponder about such subjects. Spiritual knowledge gives the soul inner strength and freedom from dependencies and fears. And this was definitely against what established ideologies and dogmas wanted people to have.

The law of karma says that everything we think, do and express is bound to generate a return in equal intensity. It is this that keeps the wheel of life in constant motion. Karmic accounts are seen as being quickly created and taking time to become settled.

The value of this natural arrangement or invisible order is that it is responsible for recording and rewarding the expression of human energy on this planet. No effort is lost; everything has meaning and creates resonance. It is refreshing to know that we can always begin anew, planting new seeds for future harvests. This is also a compelling way to learn about individual responsibility. We can't escape the consequences of our actions—nor of our inaction.

At the time of reaping good fortune, all of us enjoy encountering our destinies. Yet life today is becoming ever more unpredictable, and the fact that we have basic things like health, clarity and some ability to sustain ourselves is already a sign of very fortunate karma.

Because at this time great part of our human family is carrying an invisible burden, the practical manifestation of our will is not as easy as we would like it to be. In certain moments you may feel as if something is not quite right even though you did your best, or that your energy is blocked and things don't come to fruition. Even though focus and positive thinking are essential in keeping the mind stable, some things do take time to take form and there might be cases where they never will. Karma is free will and pre-determination working together.

We can understand life as an interplay of energies—spiritual, mental and physical. Whether we are conscious or not, a constant interaction and exchange of vibrations is being created and experienced by each of us at every moment. To be sensible and discerning before acting means you're living your *dharma*—you're acting with awareness.

The only way out is within

As souls, we are beings of light. We have come from a dimension of light, and the most powerful spiritual experiences we can have are those in the incorporeal stage, in union with the Highest Being.

Connecting with the Divine is also the means for becoming gradually liberated from one's karmic debts, for deep meditative states relieve us from the heavy baggage stored in our subconscious minds. Over time, with constant attention, we are able to clear the shadows within.

On the other hand, as long as we keep acting under the influence of our limited perceptions we continue to cause agitation in our emotional selves and in the environment. We keep losing precious energy.

The more we educate ourselves to use spiritual powers and elevate our consciousness, the more we let go of old patterns of defensiveness and aggression. Learning to see problems in a new light is always liberating. We are empowered by developing tolerance and acceptance of situations as they come and by trying to understand their roots. This world may then be seen as a stage, a creative ground, where we souls are just actors expressing ourselves through thoughts, words and actions.

There is benefit hidden in everything

There are no mistakes, no coincidences, no accidents, no sudden catastrophes. This is a cause and effect world.

Yehuda Berg

Once we go into the depths of karmic dynamics, it becomes clear that everything happens for a reason. There will of course continue to be situations we would rather not be part of. But with understanding we go through obstacles differently, with the aim of settling them. And once they are finished, we emerge lighter, as if purified in that area. This internal attitude helps in transforming our inner feelings and gives a more positive approach to life. We understand that often it is by reaping the results of past mistakes that deep internal realizations can occur. Instead of deprivation or punishment, we can choose to see difficulties as corrective events.

This is actually the hidden meaning in suffering for our actions—they may actually be the means for making us humbler, even wiser, by giving us the chance to ponder and choose better next time. Understanding karma means to break free from the bondage of living in denial as victims of fate. It gives us the feeling of living in truth, no matter how hard the circumstances. This is again living your *dharma*—to be straight on the path of righteous values.

In India, the destiny we've already created for ourselves is called *prarabdha* karma, or that which is currently bearing fruit. That does not mean you cannot create change, but rather that our life situation—health, relationships and work, among other things—can always be endured with dignity. Reacting negatively would mean, after all, creating more burdens. No matter the situation, we can always be internally free; our consciousness can remain untouched. This is another benefit of meditation—it not only creates awareness, but it empowers and sustains us like nothing else.

So, we may at times have to forgive ourselves or others; we may have to tolerate and forget. Things happen suddenly, so we had better be ready. Nothing, however, is too big or difficult when we have the foundation of understanding. God's helping hand and power are the means for guiding our boats through the rough waters of life.

Traveling in Space and Light

*Become a star
Join the company of Ra
and sail with him across the sky
in his boat of millions of years...*

The Egyptian Book of the Dead

Akash is the Sanskrit word for ether or sky, the fifth and most subtle of the elements found in nature. It pervades space and is a medium for the propagation of electromagnetic waves of sounds and visions. Just as sound vibrations travel through the air, thoughts travel through ether. In esoteric schools, *akash* is considered the storehouse of information of all that exists, available to be accessed through higher states of consciousness.

This word also appears in the Sanskrit word for radio, *akashvani*—"the sound that comes through ether." Ether is clearly not a living entity, yet it possesses properties of storage and propagation.

Another meaningful word is the one for television—*doordarshan*—which means "seeing what is distant."

These physical devices have a natural counterpart in the inner powers or natural abilities of the human soul. Ancient stories and scriptures tell of a time when people could naturally receive and send messages through thought waves and have insights of events happening in distant places, in the past or future. Intuitive faculties—including inner vision, or the faculty of clairvoyance—are not a surreal subject for a meditator. When practiced regularly over a period of time, meditation and spiritual development bring clarity, accurate intuition and at times a return of such capacities.

In this respect, there is yet another beautiful word—*sakaash*, meaning light, as in "enlightened". In spiritual vocabulary, this is the energy emanated by the Divine.

God's purest light can be stored within our souls and be felt or seen by sensitive people. It is *sakaash* that illuminates our subtle bodies and strengthens our mind fields, giving focus and clarity to our intellectual abilities. Once the mind is stable, this energy can be sent out to others through concentrated thoughts and pure feelings. In this way we might act as transmitters of God's healing powers to benefit people and nature.

In India, the first inhabitants of earth have been remembered as *devtas*—the shining ones. In fact, remembrance of elevated ancestors is a common feature of all ancient civilizations, many of which managed to preserve their stories and fables over generations. Their ways of living were later deemed sacred and their images are still found in many temples.

There is a vision of ancient history which tells of a lost civilization and a time of harmony and joy, a true Paradise, believed to be the peak of human existence. This perspective is now returning as research and findings seem to be confirming what the ancients knew so well. Old accounts speak about this period when divinized beings walked upon this earth. They later came to be known as "deities" and are usually portrayed with halos of light and royal symbols. They are believed to be God's original creation.

Spiritual Healing
Inner life, inner levels

The sovereignty of nature has been allotted to the silent forces. The moon makes not the faintest echo of a noise, yet it draws millions of tons of tidal waters to and fro at its bidding. We do not hear the sun rise nor the planets set. So, too, the dawning of the greatest moment in a man's life comes quietly, with none to herald it to the world. In that stillness alone is born the knowledge of the soul. The gliding of the mind's boat into the lagoon of the spirit is the gentlest thing I know; it is more hushed than the fall of eventide.

Paul Brunton – *The Secret Path*

Vibrational medicine has its roots in antiquity and is now becoming increasingly popular. Systems such as homeopathy, acupuncture, Ayurveda, flower remedies and energy healing are able to effectively enter a field that western traditional medicine is not even aware of. We may call it "the subtle field", and understand it as the matrix of our physical body.

Once we begin to experience the benefits of meditation and conscious living, we feel positive changes in mind and body. As a result of increased mental stability and a rise in self-esteem and confidence, we feel internally stronger. We also become more sensitive to things we are in touch with, such as the food we eat. This happens because the subtle energies of both body and mind are being purified.

The deepest form of healing happens when we connect with God in the state of soul consciousness. Even though such experiences take place in a deep state of concentration, they are strengthened and sustained by actively engaging the intellect with spiritual knowledge. By making use of spiritual understanding and perspective in our daily routine we begin to realize their value.

When the divine intellect is in command, both our personality traits and will remain aligned, in addition to other "levels" which we may call subconscious traits and past personalities. When we are linked in yoga, God's light can do its work of purifying, empowering and healing.

The more we are filled with new energy, the more we naturally think about maintaining that sense of lightness and well-being we've experienced in meditation. We begin to see value in things like taking time to meditate in the early morning or having healthy food and company. A clear picture of our inner world begins to emerge, and our strengths and true needs get a chance to become known. Love and other qualities, along with our blockages in expressing them, can then be dealt with from a position of safety.

What often happens in that stage is that we learn that many of our difficulties and illnesses are residues of things that have their roots in our past. Energy healing therapies usually deal with the more subtle levels, or energy bodies, that carry such information.

Going Deeper

The soul is the self, consciousness in the form of a spark of light, the living entity who takes the support of a brain to function in the physical dimension. Being eternal, the spirit continues to live and undergo changes through its cycle of births and rebirths. To express itself in the material world, the soul makes use of this fantastic complex of intertwined energies we call "the body". Every time we are reborn, the tiny soul brings a baggage of impressions, personal traits and karmic lessons from previous lives. The input of genetic characteristics inherited from parents and ancestors is then added in each new birth.

The body, however, has its own dynamics. The soul lives inside layers and layers of energy bodies, looking a bit like an onion skin, which in turn opens up into other layers, which together form what looks like a material body. While the body may appear as solid as brick, and layers or subtle bodies may be compared to vapor, the soul—the core being—is so tiny that it is impossible to measure it with any physical device.

The body-mind field is therefore a complete system held together by a perfect dynamic, interpenetrated by vortices or centers of energy called chakras. Every soul comes to this world with a preformed set of personality traits and a body to match whatever memories and records it carries, which will be fit for the lessons the soul has to learn. This forms the basis from which we develop in this life.

These layers or energy bodies have a frequency of their own according to the memories they carry. This means that the past is often still vibrating inside us. Even though memories may be latent and not fully conscious, they are charged with energy that may be harmonious or not. When we are able to concentrate on God, his love is able to reach deep within the soul and over time effectively heal those parts that are not integrated and still in need of change.

Vibrational medicine may be of help in this process, for it is not only effective in treating a number of illnesses but also in aiding subconscious memories which may carry mental blocks. Take homeopathy for example, where higher potencies of remedies make them capable of influencing and helping "cleaning up" the emotional body. Scientifically, it is still not known how this is achieved, for in that degree of dilution there is nothing left of the original substance except its genetic memory. This seems to point to the power of the infinitesimal, even in nature, and it is also a reminder that everything begins in the invisible.

In these times of rapid change, we benefit enormously from looking inward and seeing what is deep within the self. We souls have known and unknown blocks that exist because of unresolved situations or traumas from the past. Let´s say someone was wounded in a war or had a prolonged illness in another lifetime. The area of a past wound may show malformed subtle tissue from birth because of subtle scars in the etheric and astral bodies. This is neither visible to the eye nor can it be found in clinical tests, but it is a vulnerable spot where an illness can develop. It might also be a breach for negative influences on our energetic field. It is known that the bondages of karma are invisible and manifest in the physical, emotional and mental levels.

We have energetic circuits on these energy bodies through the levels of the chakras, through which we exchange not only physical but also emotional and mental energy with others.

To add to the complexity, we have past personalities and subconscious traits that are not integrated in the self and can at times act in almost autonomous ways. The Swiss psychiatrist Carl Jung was a pioneer in the study of what he called complexes, and he compared our psyche to an archipelago with a number of disconnected islands.

Our subconscious has a great influence and impact on our emotions because it is the basis of the subtle mechanism of thoughts and feelings. Once we learn to become internalized, we begin noticing these connections and get glimpses of areas where old personalities, or past life traits, can at times create imbalances.

This is the reason self-transformation does not happen faster, even when we want to change. We might say we carry many selves, one wishing one thing, the other demanding something else. Deep within the unconscious mind, there are parts that resist change and wage war. All spiritual paths talk about the battle with Maya—the hold that negativity and old mental habits have on the self.

Now we can see why a higher force is crucial in our endeavors to succeed, together with a good dose of determination. We have been trying to change ourselves and the course of history for a long time without the support of spiritual love. It is love that sustains our efforts and takes us beyond the blocks and obstacles that appear from time to time. If for some reason or another we don't experience attainments in our spiritual journey—basic things like inner peace and love—we tend to stop making efforts after a few difficulties on the path. We end up forgetting that learning to overcome difficulties means gaining inner strength and freedom.

Past Lives

Imagine someone who lived like a king and is now living an uneventful life or has become a kind of a beggar. The soul may unconsciously refuse or be unaware of how to live in scarcity, or maybe insist on sustaining attitudes which are only imaginary. In the world we live in today we rarely find someone totally satisfied and happy, and people are visibly becoming emotionally impoverished.

Lots of unconscious energy is drained when parts of us do not see or accept the trials of our present existence. Though a king is a radical example, most of us have past personalities that may be as strong in their ideas and as a result end up polarizing our consciousness, creating imbalance. Scientists say we do not use our brain´s capacity as we could. In energy healing work, this has been seen as one of the reasons why this happens.

While psychiatry may call it "dissociation" or "multiple personalities" syndrome, the fact is that most of us have at least a strong double, or shadow. It may sometimes appear clothed in the ego, trying to impose its desires and claims. We could compare our energy fields to a spiritual condominium in which a number of past selves live together, not always satisfied with the company of their neighbors.

Soul consciousness is a powerful method for concentrating the energy of our will and reinforcing our qualities, which then align and naturally cool internal disorders down. The qualities of humility and discipline have always been regarded as the basis of spiritual development. One needs to have determination in order to conquer negativities, which are far more complex and deep-rooted than we imagine. We also need a good deal of patience and faith in our own process of transformation.

Having worked as a volunteer in an energy healing group, I had the chance to observe how past personalities manifest and influence our present. Past attitudes may sometimes be so radically different from the present persona that their expression catches everyone by surprise. At times it looked as if someone else has entered the energy field. Yet once you are trained to discern, you know it is usually a facet of the person´s past that takes the chance to emerge.

Because they are mostly unconscious, these repressed and often un-integrated personas may not be bound by the body they inhabit. In cases where they are stronger than the present personality, they may be the cause behind strong depression or mental illnesses.

In fact, it may happen that part of us may still be subtly caught up in the events of our past or holding on to karmic situations of which we are not even aware. Something similar happens in family circles where souls are often brought together for a chance to settle past debts and create a harmonious relationship this time around.

As we enter the invisible territory called the quantum field, we experience things as being deeply connected. Here, the more we know, the more we become aware of the need to integrate our many facets and open up to deep spiritual healing.

Positive Vibrations

We live in a period of transformation and great discoveries. While consciousness continues to be a mystery for mainstream science, there are pioneering works studying its manifestations.

The positive side to know about the inner diversity we carry is that we can more clearly recognize hidden talents and strengths that may just be reawakening. For our past lives might also have been good, even extraordinary. Let´s say one has worked on the self, gained wisdom, used authority well, worked for the welfare of humanity, etc. This energy is still vibrating within the self, still sustaining and influencing the present, even if only subtly.

What happens through a relationship with God is that he can see and reinforce our best, and he finds ways to inspire and use our qualities. By knowing our complete story, he may wish to make use of our gifts and connections for the spiritual development and support of others. As we have seen, one of his main roles is as *Karankaravanhar*—the One who gets work done through others.

The spiritual journey is therefore as important as the final destination of becoming complete with qualities and inner powers, as well as free of karmic bondages.

Our consciousness is now known to be multidimensional and capable of operating on a number of levels. By being unlimited in his potential, the Supreme Soul can truly heal, sustain and empower us. He may also use us in the service of humanity if we are ready. One just needs to be open-hearted and keep receiving his ever-benevolent and powerful Light.

Walk your journey in Silence

There is no merit higher than Yoga, no good higher than Yoga, no subtlety higher than Yoga; there is nothing that is higher than Yoga.

Yogasikha-Upanishad I.67

As we elevate our consciousness and begin to grow spiritually we become aware of the energy that surrounds us—the vibrations we create and spread out into the world. Things like the food we eat; the cleanliness of our bodies, homes and clothes; and our habits of thinking and speaking may boost or diminish our spiritual energy. Every little thing, every thought produces energy that rebounds and sustains or damages us. At this level, everything counts.

We have seen a few connections between God's energy and love and how spiritual knowledge and yoga have the potential for triggering deep change in our lives. For this to ring true, we need to try to experiment ourselves.

Connecting with the Divine is an easy way of attaining stability of mind and developing spiritual intelligence and clear intuition. These are some of the attainments of Raja Yoga. Yet for God´s light to keep constantly reaching and fulfilling the soul, we have to continue to refine our energy and thoughts through study and meditation.

Purity and Love
Know yourself, free yourself

Inner purity is the closest thing to freedom we can experience in life. It is the capacity of being present with your whole being yet totally uninvolved in terms of judgment and expectation. Our capacity to feel and express love is also based on purity. The soul's channels can then remain open, no matter what or who is surrounding it.

Purity as a virtue has become often misunderstood, when not looked down on, in a world driven by self-interest, ego and competition. Yet it will always be the basis from which all other qualities develop, together with conscious awareness and inner values. Besides, it places one in a position of boldness and strength in a world filled with mediocrity and waste.

To sustain this inner stage, we need discipline. The intellect and mind need to be stimulated and strengthened by churning concepts of truth as well as by experiencing contrasts in life. When there is awareness, there will always be a new lesson to assimilate. In this regard, one of the first things a yogi learns is to deliberately look for qualities in those he or she meets, as well as in situations, as opposed to looking at defects. This becomes a means of transforming circumstances.

Here, what begins as an exercise may develop into a new habit. If we pick up the good aspects, we see meaning in situations and do not get frustrated or lose our temper. It is not that you do not see problems or difficulties but that even while seeing them, you do not focus on nor get affected by them. By being emotionally unaffected, it is easier to reconcile opposites or find a solution.

To have benevolent feelings and see virtues is a refined art. Just as people are determined in their defects, the yogi may well remain as determined in seeing virtues. Besides benefitting others, this is also a means of protecting the self. When we relate to others based on their virtues, we end up developing those virtues ourselves.

I remember a very special woman who spent her life being stable in her inner stage of purity. One of the most striking things about her was that everyone felt they could talk to her about anything. Her power as the head of a huge spiritual organization was exercised in a gentle manner. Maybe to an outsider she was a bit naïve, a leader who did not hold authority in a worldly sense. Yet if you saw the effect she had on people, you'd think otherwise.

Because she was internally clean, whatever she said resonated and created impact. People changed in her company. Outwardly, her simplicity and goodness were visible, but it was her company, her purity that created transformation. Her honesty was developed by remaining close to God all her life. She had assimilated his energy, and you could feel it.

In the spiritual dimension, our presence and words only have an impact when our mind is powerful. And this is another aspect of purity—it not only brings us closer to God's own nature, but it serves to contain and maximize the powers we receive from him. Purity is the sign of a noble soul.

Becoming Yogis

Two things are required before Grace manifests itself in man. One is the capacity to receive it. The other is cooperation with it. For the first, he must humble the ego; for the second, he must purify it.

Paul Brunton – *Secret India*

Sadhana is the determination and focus we need for self-development, the kind of subtle effort that becomes part of one's thoughts, life and routine. Most people dislike the very thought of discipline. It sounds heavy, forced; almost synonymous with coercion. For a yogi, discipline has a lot to do with taking care of one's mind. This means we are responsible for creating and sustaining our inner stage—our mood—always. In simple terms, whenever we feel that something is not right, we think of practical methods to transform it.

For example, let's say you're feeling a bit down or frustrated. Before letting sadness settle in, you take necessary action. It might be that your inner self needs to be cared for and understood; it might be that just by listening to music you love or singing, you let it go. The fact is, you're aware and tending to the inner workings of your mind.

This is something we learn to develop. And here comes another aspect of discipline, for I have seen this succeed more easily in the context of group work. I had a few thoughts when trying to find out why.

When a group of like-minded individuals connect for a higher purpose, an energy field is created. The Greeks called it *egregore*. The more people's thoughts and activities are harmonious, the more the gathering becomes a network of sharing, sustenance and service.

Once we begin developing spiritually we start to gain confidence and inner powers—it might be new enthusiasm and creativity, tolerance, the capacity to discern and so on. It won't take long for us to realize that the biggest challenge on the path always has to do with one's own ego and desires. These may be expressed in various forms—old habits and concepts, the ways we like things to be done, the things we expect from others—whether it is recognition or help. The list is long because we are talking about human nature in our time.

It may also happen that at a certain point one feels stuck for some reason and not able to move forward. There will be opposing forces too, both internal and external. We live in a society that is not designed or conducive to spiritual development; there are times when you feel you're swimming against the current. It is at this point that you might feel the benefit of belonging.

Those who are together for the purpose of spiritual growth also give us an idea of our progress. In this holographic world, everyone is a mirror, which means we can always see ourselves in others if we want to. This is an exercise of the intellect and works as an opportunity to see what is reflected back to us. Tests and obstacles will continue to come from all sides, including from those in the group. Yet seeing the way more mature people develop consciousness and deal with difficulties becomes a great way for us to learn how to act and handle things in a practical way.

The more our awareness grows and we accumulate new energy, the more we feel able to give support to others. This giving is another blessing, for it is also the means of our own sustenance. To be of service to others is a great chance to improve our karmic situation, it is a fortune we can always create and it doesn't necessarily need to be something visible. Our role in the community might be that of giving support through our inner work and presence, for example. The same is true with the opposite. What we do, even when no one sees, may bring different kinds of damage to the energy-field of the group.

Another positive thing about being part of a gathering has to do with a constancy that we may sometimes lack when alone on the path. Even for those who meditate often, it´s far too easy to get disconnected and lose oneself in this world of distractions. "Maya" is the Sanskrit word that defines the illusions created by things that consume our energy and distort our perception. Over time, the soul weakens, and feelings of powerlessness may take over. It is at this point that the love of someone else—his or her closeness to God—may bring back the Light that for a moment was extinguished.

To have like-minded friends or a good support group is something we might like to consider if we are determined to develop spiritually. Even though our *sadhana* will always remain individual, the gathering is a place for exchanging love and sustenance. And there are days when we certainly need it.

Yaguia — the Sacrificial Fire

The combined influence and wisdom of a group is more powerful than that of an individual. By lighting another candle, we do not diminish the original flame; we only make the light brighter and stronger.

Yehuda Berg

It is with great love that I remember those who took the first steps on the spiritual path I have chosen as my own. It was around the mid-1930s when a community in the province of the then Indian Sindh was shaken by strange and powerful events. What was beginning there not only defied traditional customs and established views of religion, it also created a spiritual revolution that few predicted would grow and expand the way it did. It was all centered around a man named Dada Lekhraj.

Being a family man, a devoted Hindu and a pillar of his wealthy community, Dada never harbored feelings of becoming a spiritual teacher. In fact, his own quest for truth took him to adopt more than a dozen gurus over time. As he matured in life, he felt ever more drawn into solitude and began to have experiences that none of his gurus were able to explain. It came to a point where their frequency started to disturb his business routine.

Dada began to experience powerful waves of transcendent love and bliss, and the more he felt inclined to retire into solitude to experience them, the more the same vibrations started to be felt by others. While most of these people were from his community, a few others came from distant places. They were drawn together through vibrations and subtle visions. Something was happening—not because of him, but through him. Yet nobody knew what it was.

Their First Belief

Interestingly enough, these experiences were felt mostly by girls and young women who were "touched" by spiritual love and inner visions. It did not take long for a small group to form around Dada.

For some time, their spiritual practice consisted in reading a few verses of scriptures and chanting a mantra that took the mind into silence. Chanting "*Om*" was enough for them to disconnect from the outside world and have the most extraordinary experiences. They not only felt deep inner peace and waves of magic bliss, but they were taken to other realms where they were shown that the ancient past was connected with the near future.

Together with the beauty of a new world, they began "seeing" events that they believed would unfold in their lifetime. All this was shocking news to the traditional clan of Brahmins to which Dada belonged.

Because all this happened in altered states of consciousness, they were at first not able to know or recognize the true nature and origin of those things. It would take years and a number of situations for them to learn that a greater power was involved and was in fact the source of their experiences.

That early time later became known as the period of visions, when all they had was direct experience and hardly any knowledge. That initial group became known as "Om Mandali"—the circle of *Om*—and would later unfold into a path of revealed knowledge and a renaissance of spiritual yoga.

The initial core group became the foundation for a gathering of powerful yogis, who were later called the Brahma Kumaris—"the spiritual daughters of Brahma". Their disciplined lifestyle was based on purity and renunciation, with the aim of working on themselves. Their inner lives blossomed as they remained together for fourteen years before beginning their mission of service.

Their story still continues. Though Dada is no longer among us, he left a legacy of unlimited love and determination, becoming a living example of all aspects of self-transformation. Today, those young girls are in their eighties and nineties. They became accomplished yoginis, manifesting in their lives the *shaktis*—powers—of the Creator. They have become instrumental in changing the lives of millions of people around the world.

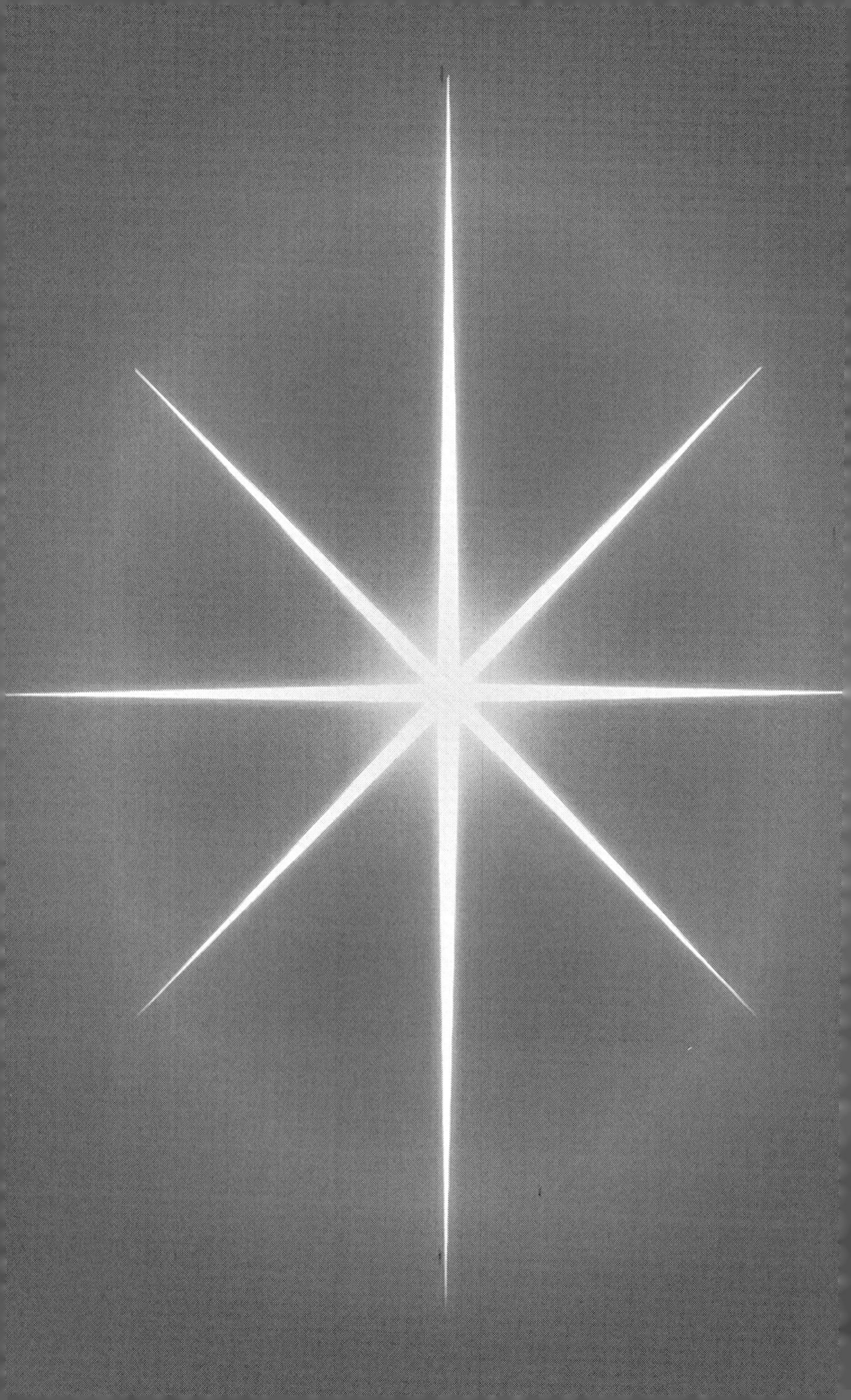

Beginning Meditation

First thing you should know as you sit for meditation — you're not doing anything new. You're just using your capacity to focus and to remember things that belong to your original nature. It should be easy and relaxing, never a struggle. This is not a practice to suppress thoughts or emotions, but to transform them. You'll be creating elevated thoughts until you come to a point of stillness, where there are just good feelings and a sense of inner fulfillment.

Your connection with God is part of your soul story. The time might just be right for you both to reconnect more closely. Have the awareness that you're going to meet an old friend. Let pure feelings guide your thoughts and you'll be surprised how easily you get to feel his presence.

You may begin with a silent conversation from the heart. If you have any burdens or concerns, give them to him first. You may write him if you like. It is important to unburden the self first so that you feel relieved from worries and can be open to the meditation experience.

If you're a visual kind of person, you can use a point of light image to focus on. It may help you to concentrate when you are beginning. Keep your eyes slightly open during meditation—it will help you to stabilize and not let your mind stray. Let some gentle instrumental music play in the background to raise your spirits and create an atmosphere.

Becoming soul conscious means experimenting with thoughts of being light, being an eternal spirit. Remember that everything that is connected to the body image—the present personality, shape, color, etc.—belongs to a temporary role you're playing. You're the actor who is making the body function; the conscious being who is now getting in touch with spiritual reality, with your inner qualities and powers. If you feel this with sincerity, deep within, your energy will start to rise. You'll feel lighter in body and mind.

Remember your Father of Light. Talk to him. Share your love. Enjoy his presence and the feelings and powers he will shower on your inner self.

Tips for Meditation and Spiritual Development

As we know, there are no results without effort. If you really plan to get the most out of your meditation, it helps to understand that there are methods that work as a foundation. Raja Yoga is based on remembering who you are, and from that stage, connecting with the Source. You can do it anytime, anywhere, for it simply means "remembrance". Yet there are things that facilitate the process and speed up our progress.

Try to set a time to have a regular practice. Once you get into a routine, the mind will be naturally pulled into that state. Discipline is the basis of spiritual development.

Try to live in a clean environment and be clean in your body and clothing. Showering before meditation, for example, makes a difference.

There are times of the day when meditating is easier, and one can more easily flow into deeper experiences. The early morning is the most powerful time. You remain positive throughout the day when you do it. Sunset or any time around 7 p.m. in the evening is another good moment, for you can tune into the waves of thousands of meditators who are also connecting at that time.

Sit in a comfortable position; use a chair if necessary. The important thing is to be at ease with your body; to have your back straight but not strained. Try to keep your eyes slightly open; once you concentrate you'll see that it helps you not to get distracted or sleepy.

Studying or reading some inspirational material is always good, for it helps to inspire, focus and give the mind a direction. There are times when you might want to sit with an aim in mind, such as "today I'd like to experience peace" or "today I'd like to experience love" and so on.

Take short breaks during the day, even if only for a minute, to connect your mind to the One. This will help you remain focused and avoid waste thoughts. It will also give you the feeling of having a relationship.

Having a corner or a meditation room will help create and sustain a spiritual vibration in your house. You'll feel that that is your place of deep peace and nurturing. Sitting there in the morning and at the end of the day will become a pleasure.

The way we spend our day greatly influences the experience we get in meditation. Being linked in yoga and light in self and relationships, we flow into experiences more easily. Days spent in concern or unnecessary thoughts will make it harder. Watching this connection will make you value your meditation even more. You'll see that it helps us to be more aware as we go through things.

Live like a lotus; in other words, it doesn't matter what the situation is around you—try your best to remain untouched by its negative aspects. Do not repress, but try to understand things with your heart and use your qualities to nurture yourself and others.

Dedicate a day to cleaning your room, office and home from time to time. Accumulating old things like clothes, shoes, paper and objects you don't use keeps the energy in your house stagnant. The more you are light within, the more you are happy with less.

Keep track of how you earn and use your resources—body, mind and wealth are important, as they are different types of energy in our lives.

Natural resources are also important as we live in a time when wasting water, for example, can lead to scarcity. Knowing that every action produces a reaction or consequence makes us more careful. Be charitable if you can, but understanding the way in which your donation will be used is also important.

If you're serious about refining your energy and evolving spiritually, watching what you eat is essential. A vegetarian diet is appropriate for a yogi for obvious reasons. You may want to inform yourself about it.

Keep a diary in which you can note important milestones in your progress. Things like small changes in attitude (beginning to see virtues instead of focusing on defects, for example) and being concerned about making the soul beautiful will give you an extra boost in life.

As much as you give and receive love, also have a gentle but firm conversation with yourself from time to time. Teach your mind the right ways and tell it how keeping negative traits will only result in more suffering.

Whenever there is a challenging situation or external problem, consider meditating for longer periods, or at least more frequently. Remembrance is a powerful tool for overcoming all types of obstacles.

Once you begin to remove certain blocks from your mind, you'll see qualities emerging that are ready to be used. When you let go of laziness, for example, you'll see new enthusiasm or energy arising as if out of nowhere. Beneath all weaknesses, there are inner powers waiting to be reawakened.

Look at your shadow with truth and mercy. Never be afraid of being yourself. God loves you and he never loses hope in you, no matter what.

Regain your self-esteem through the love of God. Just open yourself to his eternal love and your love will begin to flow again.

To walk with dignity and independence in this life, be disciplined, focused and detached. Have long-term vision in actions and relationships.

Truth and cleanliness—both inner and outer—have a lot in common. As we continue to live in truth, challenging situations will be sorted out automatically.

Be in contact with nature. Try not to watch as much TV for a while and see what happens to your mind. Create new experiences; try pursuing art and forming new relationships with like-minded people. Sometimes we have to break from old habits in order to create new ones.

Company has a big influence on our inner stage and vibrations. Be a good friend to yourself in the first place and you'll also be a good friend to others. Unnecessary criticism and gossiping are of no benefit to anyone.

Be selective with what you feed your mind and body. Waste thoughts rob us of precious time and energy. Try not to be concerned about what others are doing or saying unless you have a responsibility to. Focus on the self.

In India they say: "do not give sorrow, do not take sorrow". Try to be of service to others and you will feel that God will be able to use your virtues, talents and gifts.

Good wishes and pure feelings always work like magic. Likewise, the more blessings we receive from others, the higher we fly.

There is a connection between spiritual strength and lightness. Thoughts may also be "heavy", so we had better choose them carefully. The more we act consciously and give our worries to God, the more we remain carefree and light.

About the Authors

Simone Boger is a Brazilian freelance writer and yogini, who lived and worked for many years in India and other countries. She began her spiritual journey early, having practiced and taught meditation for the past 28 years. Her previous book — *The Cycle of Time* — explores the links between ancient history and spirituality, and can be accessed on her website: <www.cycleoftime.com>

Shilo Shiv Suleman is an Indian illustrator, animator and visual artist based in the city of Bangalore. Her beautiful and inspiring work can be seen on her blog: <http://bonifisheii.blogspot.com>

For updated information, book excerpts and meditation videos, please visit the Facebook page: https://www.facebook.com/ThePowerOfLovebook

Made in the USA
Charleston, SC
17 May 2014